By Mopar
to the
Golden Gate

A 50 year old car
on a 100 year old road

DENNY GIBSON

ACKNOWLEDGMENTS

Big thanks to John Nawrocki for sharing the driving at the trip's beginning and risking life and limb while taking the Lincoln Tunnel picture from the back seat. I really appreciate John Peters allowing me to use the photo he took of Abraham, Denny, & John in Bucyrus and I'm thankful to Carolee Wheeler for photos of the Valiant in the wild wild west. Thanks also to my son, Crispian, for taking the pictures in Lincoln Park.

Laurel Kane's much appreciated proofreading has saved me from bunches of embarrassment.

A large amount of credit for this book even existing belongs to Brian Butko for convincing me that self publishing was easy and honorable. It definitely feels honorable and modern technology has indeed made publishing much easier than ever before though it might still be a stretch to call it easy. Brian's further help with proofreading, advise, encouragement, and even some photo editing has been invaluable.

Contents

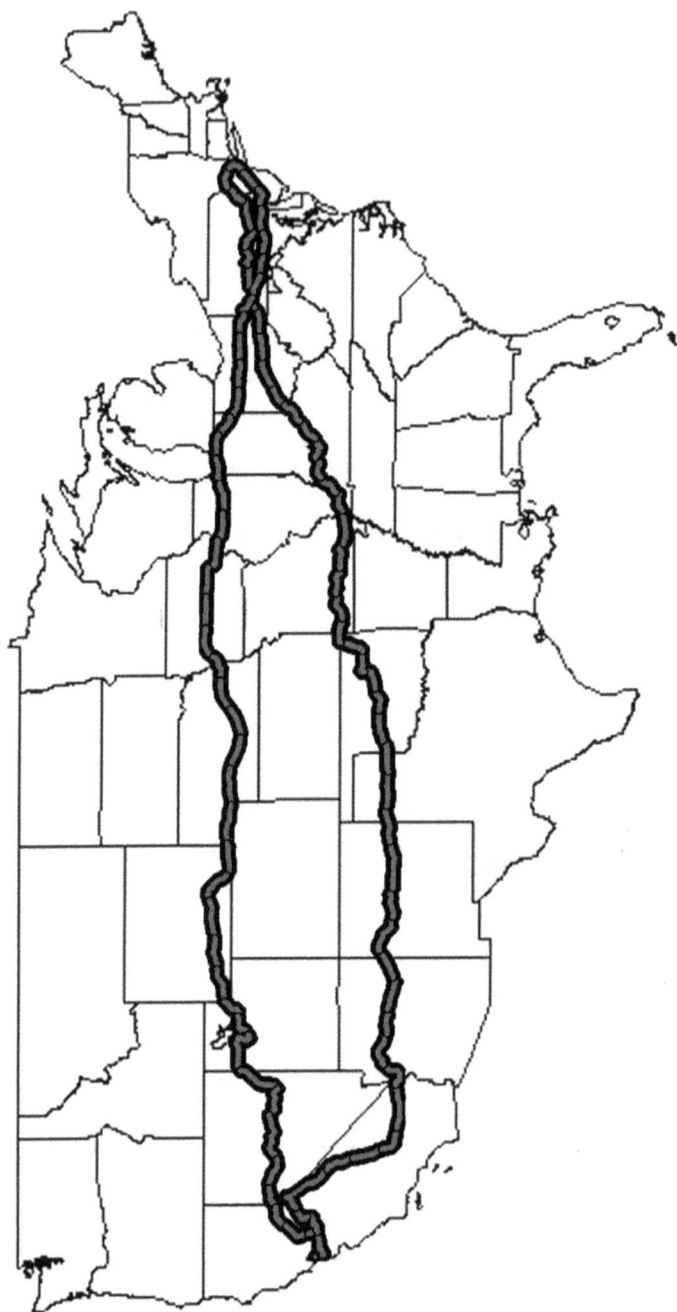

All the way (and then some) on the Lincoln Highway

1 AN IDEA COMETH

Many will recognize this book's title as a take on Emily Post's *By Motor to the Golden Gate*. That book, published in 1916, recounted one of the earliest motorcar journeys between New York City and San Francisco. This book recounts one of the most recent. When Post did it, the Lincoln Highway, as a concept, was just a few years old and, as a reality, was still rather vague in spots. When I did it, the concept of the Lincoln Highway had reached a hundred years of age. The reality of it had pretty much come and gone and it was once again rather vague in spots.

When the Lincoln Highway turned ninety in 2003, an official Lincoln Highway Association caravan travelled it from end to end. I was aware of the caravan and a little jealous of the lucky participants but it was nothing I seriously considered being part of. For one thing, my day job simply would not permit me to run around the country for weeks at a time. For another, my love affair with old roads was not yet fully formed. It, too, was still rather vague in spots.

I started, or, in some sense, restarted, taking road trips in 1999 after my nest had gone empty. A full length drive of Route 66 was followed by an attempt to retrace a trip my great-grandparents had made in 1920. An interest in old and historic roads started to surface. I drove pieces of the National Road, the Dixie Highway, and the Lincoln Highway. I drove Sixty-Six again. I drove the National Road end-to-end and more pieces of the Lincoln and Dixie. The idea of driving the Lincoln Highway end-to-end in one go, like those 2003 caravaners did, started to form and targeting the centennial year of 2013 seemed natural.

A few of the cars that made the drive in 2003 were late model modern vehicles but most were not. Several were from the period, 1910s and 1920s, when the Lincoln Highway was at its peak and the rest of the twentieth century was well represented as well. All of my road trips were made in cars just a few years old. Sure, they were comfortable and reliable but maybe I ought to try something different for the centennial. Maybe something more in keeping with the spirit of that ninetieth anniversary caravan.

I immediately thought of driving a one hundred year old car over the one hundred year old route but discarded the idea almost as quickly as it came to me. Procuring a 1913 model something would be challenging but not quite impossible; maintaining it on a cross country drive just might be. So what about a car from the Lincoln's heyday? Perhaps a nice 1920s Model A. That was much more realistic and I don't think I ever consciously ruled it out but, before it ever really took hold, I had a "better" idea.

Maybe a car exactly as old as the Lincoln Highway was beyond my means and maintenance abilities but perhaps I could manage one half as old. Cars built in 1963 would turn 50 when the Highway turned 100 and that wasn't the only thing significant about the year. 1963 was the year I got my driver's license and the year I bought my first car. Driving something that appeared in a new car show room just as I was getting my first taste of mobility was attractive. The idea grew on me quickly. By sometime in 2007 or maybe even 2006, I'd pretty much settled on 1963 as the model year of the car I would someday buy and drive across the United States.

2 TAKES FORM

The idea remained just an idea for several years. I occasionally looked over online listings and poked around a few car shows but I was not seriously shopping. I was refining my shopping list.

I decided that I probably ought to have the car in hand two or three years before the trip. There seemed a pretty good chance that any car my budget allowed would need significant preparation time. A couple of years would allow for an engine rebuild or similar work if necessary. Assuming that the trip would occur in the middle of 2013, I should make my buy by the middle of 2010 or 2011.

Refining the shopping list involved something of a rehash of automotive history. There were some really cool cars around in 1963. It was the first year of the Corvette Stingray and the Buick Riviera. It was the second (and final) year of the Studebaker Avanti and the third year of the Jaguar XKE. It was the third (and final) year for those cool looking rocket ship shaped third generation Thunderbirds. All of these were attractive and some were even a little tempting but none were really in my price range. I did see advertisements for a couple of Avantis and a T-bird or two whose purchase I might have managed but whose care and feeding could have put my ability to buy groceries at risk. Besides, most of those cool cars were not (with the exception of the XKE) cars that I really wanted to own.

The early 1960s were when some smaller cars started to appear and that's really where my interest lay. Volkswagen Beetles were quite popular then and one would certainly have been an interesting ride. However I felt that driving the premier American highway on its big birthday should be done in an American car. I scratched the Beetle off the list.

But small was where my thoughts were turning and there were a number of small American cars being built in 1963. Compacts, they were called. Maybe not as small as Volkswagen Beetles but smaller than Rivieras and Thunderbirds. A smallish Rambler even carried the name American. There were Falcons, Comets, Darts, Valiants, Corvairs, Novas, Tempests, F-85s, Specials, and Larks. These were all cars that I liked and considered for the trip.

I ruled out three of the cars mentioned in the preceding paragraph because of my perception that parts would be hard to come by. The three were the Studebaker Lark, the Rambler American, and the Chevrolet Corvair. I waffled on avoiding Corvairs because I'd owned, and been very happy with, two of them. In the end, though, I knew that parts for one could be just as hard to get as for a Rambler or Studebaker. The little Buicks (Specials), Oldsmobiles (F-85s), and Pontiacs (Tempests) stayed on the list but were not at its top. The reason was volume. These three just hadn't been as popular as the others and I figured that more cars sold would mean more parts available. So, when I started getting fairly serious in the summer of 2010, I was primarily looking for Falcons, Comets, Darts, Valiants, and Novas.

There were cars on the market from all of my chosen marques. Some were beautiful show cars, some were street rods, and some were essentially projects. Lots of fifty year old cars have been totally restored to better than new condition and many times higher than new price tags. Others have been turned into racers or at least things that looked like racers. Neither of these were what I had in mind. Even if my budget had allowed it, I didn't really want to drive across the country while worrying about chipping the paint or getting dust in the diamond tufting. Nor did I want to do it with a rumbling engine and jarring suspension better suited to a drag strip. That left me with the projects.

At one end of the project car range are the piles of parts whose sellers say things like, "I think it's all there." For the most part, only highly sought after collector cars like '55 Chevys and '57 Studebaker

Hawks actually get sold like this. In fact, I don't believe I encountered any of my chosen makes of my chosen year in this condition. Of course, I wasn't looking for any so there could be a 1963 basket case Comet or some such out there that I just didn't see. At the other end, I suppose, are well maintained oldies that just recently suffered a breakdown or a collision. I say "suppose" because I did not come across any of these, either. What I did find were mostly faded specimens that suffered more from neglect than traumatic encounters or unexpected mechanical malfunctions.

I did more shopping on line than in person and I even made a few offers. Fortunately, none made the cut. I call this fortunate because cars (and other things) tend to appear much better on line than in person. I initially thought it a little surprising that two of the cars I made offers on were Mopars, i.e., Chrysler products. One Plymouth Valiant and one Dodge Dart. Actually quite a few of the cars I found legitimate candidates for my drive were Mopars. I considered this for a bit and decided it really wasn't strange at all. In 1963 there really was a Big Three in Detroit and Chrysler was as respected as any of them. In fact, many considered Chrysler to be leading the field in terms of engineering. They didn't invent the alternator but they did invent a rectifier that made it practical and were the first to make it standard in a passenger car, the 1960 Valiant. They didn't invent torsion bar suspension either (several European cars and Packards used it much earlier) but I and most of my high school class mates thought they did. No, there really wasn't anything strange at all in the fact that Darts and Valiants were showing up on my shopping radar with some frequency. Chrysler products of the 1950s and '60s were as solid as any and more innovative than many.

As the end of the year approached, a Valiant convertible caught my eye on eBay. The car was in Ohio and, after talking with the owner on the phone, I decided to take a look. But this is a good sized state and, even though I did not have to cross state lines to reach the car, I did have to cross about 160 miles of Ohio. The car was in a warehouse-like garage in a downtown area where the owner met me right on time. It was under a cover which we quickly removed. The Valiant was no pampered beauty but it seemed like it might be the right car for me.

I liked the car and I liked its story though I only know a little of it. The car was a 1963 slant six powered Valiant 200 convertible with a TorqueFlite automatic transmission. The TorqueFlite was controlled, of course, by pushbuttons which I thought was pretty cool. The fire engine red paint job was part of the story. The car's current owner believed he was the third. He had bought the car to give his ailing father something to tinker with and I believe that tinkering included repairing some fairly minor front end damage. After the tinkering was done and the father passed on, the car saw little use except for one thing, parades.

The owner was an elected city official and the little convertible made a nice parade vehicle. It was OK in its original white but would be even better in bright red and so it was done. The paint job was at least a decade old when I first saw the car but it looked very good. There were hints that it was a cut rate job but texture wasn't one of them. Apparently the radio antenna had not been masked and one side was covered by red overspray. Conversely, there was a white spot on the left that must have been masked by accident since the same spot on the other side had been nicely painted red. Fortunately, this spot was small and not at all obvious. In fact, it was visible only with the top down and would have been covered by the top boot if the car still had one. Standing on the car's right and looking at the air intake grill just in front of the windshield revealed a lot of white on the sides of the slots. The view from the left showed nothing but red. As noted, these little goofs might indicate an Earl Scheib $29.95 type paint job but everything else said otherwise. The surface was as smooth and shiny as you could want with absolutely no runs or orange peel. More importantly, that smooth paint seemed to be on top of smooth and rust free metal.

The car started right up with no smoke or gushing leaks. There were no plates on the car which ruled out a real test drive but moving the car back and forth through the forty or so feet of space in the garage gave me no reason to question the seller's stories of semi-recent drives. Even if it only had to travel a few miles in a parade once or twice a year, it required some basic maintenance to do that reliably. In between parades, it sat covered inside an unheated but quite dry enclosed space.

So, what's not to like? Well… Since it spent most of its time indoors and only went out when it was at least nice enough for folks to sit in the back and wave, there was no need for a top. It had not been removed but it had been allowed to completely deteriorate. The frame was intact and there was some cloth attached but there was no rear window and some of that attached cloth looked like it might not be attached much longer. Some front seat seams had separated and bits of carpet had rotted away. Although there were, as I said, no gushing leaks, dark spots on the floor indicated some ongoing leakage. It also seemed likely that there had been heater core leakage sometime in the past. It was completely disconnected. No need for a heater in summertime parades.

But the good outweighed the bad and the car was fairly priced. I decided this was as close as I was going to get to whatever it was I was looking for. I bought the Valiant.

1963 Valiant in Cambridge, OH, garage

3 AND GETS READY

I now owned a forty-seven year old car on the far side of the state. I returned home, got the title transferred to my name, and bought license plates. It was four days before Christmas. I anticipated taking possession of the car between Christmas and the end of the year but it ended up being the first week of January before things came together.

What came together was a friend and an idle day to drive me to the car and follow me back. During the time I'd been shopping for an old car, I got various pieces of advice from fellows with some real experience with them. One of the most common was "Don't plan on driving it home." There were just too many things to go wrong, they said. Tires, brakes, lights, hoses, belts, et cetera, et cetera. I don't question that advice in the slightest. But I did sort of brush it aside.

We did make one change in my original plans. I had proposed that Rick, the friend who had agreed to join me on the vehicle acquisition mission, drive my Vibe. My thinking was that this would inconvenience him the least. He proposed that we take his F-150 instead. His thinking was that, should things turn sour, we might be able to rent a dolly or trailer and still get the car to Cincinnati. His proposal won.

It was cloudy and damp on the day of the retrieval. In a welcome change from the recent past, the temperature was above freezing but not by a whole lot. Those warnings I'd received about driving a newly purchased antique home were all pretty generic. More specific warnings might relate to driving in the cold and damp in a vehicle without a heater or rear window or much of a roof. But I was prepared. I dug out the down parka I'd last worn in a predawn wait to see Punxsutawney Phil, grabbed the heavy gloves, and packed a warm stocking cap. We put the new plates on the Valiant, checked out a few things like lights, tires, and fluids and hit the road.

My foul weather preparation paid off and, while hardly toasty warm, I was actually fairly comfortable temperature wise. The car ran great and even drove reasonably well. Not knowing which, if any, of the symphony of unfamiliar squeaks and rattles meant something serious, I ignored them all. The brakes worked just like new. Automotive brakes have improved immensely since the early 1960s. The unassisted drum brakes on the Valiant were actually rather good for their time. They just required some extra effort and benefited from a little advance planning.

To end any suspense, the car made the trip home without a hiccup. With every mile, I began to feel a little better about my purchase. It certainly needed work but giving me 160 good miles straight away and "as is" seemed a very good sign.

Between buying the car and picking it up, I'd made preliminary arrangements for a top. Within a few days of getting the car home, I dropped it off at the upholstery shop and, by early February, a nice white top was in place. In the few miles I had driven the Valiant, I became convinced that some front end work was needed. I took the car directly from the upholstery shop, which was run by the friend of a friend, to a restoration shop run by the friend of another friend.

The Valiant getting a new top
(Photo by Bob Dane)

People who rebuild old cars often develop expertise and interest in specific makes. The fellow I'd taken the Valiant to was primarily a Chevy man with a fair amount of Ford work to his credit as well. He looked things over a bit but soon let me know he thought we would both be happier if he passed on the Valiant. He was not at all comfortable tackling the torsion bar suspension and was at a point in his career where he was not much interested in a major learning opportunity. I wasn't all that much interested in providing such an opportunity, either, so I thanked him for his candor, which I did truly appreciate, and moved the car to the friend of another friend.

This friend of a friend operates a successful and well respected garage with a few employees. I soon learned that the front end wasn't nearly as bad as I perceived. There was a tiny bit of play in the tie

rods but not enough to warrant replacing them. A simple alignment helped tremendously. It also helped being told that "It drives about like any old car." Part of the problem was just that I had forgotten what it was like to drive a mid-century

The Valiant's mechanicals get some attention

automobile with no power steering or other camouflage between the steering wheel and the road. The main cause of those spots on the floor was also eliminated during this visit by replacing the rear main seal. Doing this provided a chance to examine the crank shaft which was determined to be in pretty good shape. Some aging and brittle fuel line was also replaced.

So, the "emergency" repairs were done by mid-March and I took a break for the summer. I drove the car now and then, though never more than a hundred miles, and began to get a little familiar with it.

Shortly after buying the Valiant, I stopped by a friend's body shop. It was partly just to show off my new ride and partly to talk about possibly doing some work on the car in the future. The driver's door didn't close quite right and I thought he might be able to help. He looked it over and suggested a little realignment of the front fenders might do it. We agreed to get more serious about it at summer's end. In the fall, a closer examination revealed a deeper problem.

Here is a little non-expert background that might help make sense of this. With the 1960 and 1961 models, Chrysler switched all of its cars other than the Imperial to unibody construction. They were the first auto manufacturer to do so on such a scale. In unibodies, there is no separate full length frame and much of a car's structural strength comes from the body's sheet metal. The roof plays a big part in this except, of course, for convertibles. 1963 was the first year for a Valiant convertible which means that my car was one of the world's earliest unibody convertibles. Without the full frame or a metal roof, things can sag over time. That is exactly what had happened with my car.

My friend with the body shop suggested a friend of his with a frame shop and helped me arrange to get the car in for a look. It could be jacked into shape but it would not hold without some custom bracing. As both the friend and the friend of the friend were semi-retired and trying to be fully retired, there was zero interest in taking on such a project.

This was pretty bad news, I thought. The car was not going to break in two immediately but it might someday and closing that door sure wasn't going to get any easier. I briefly considered trying to dump the car and going back to shopping. It was a sad time.

Of course, 1963 Valiant convertibles were not the only cars ever to exhibit body sag. I somehow learned that after market bracing was available for some of the more popular cars of the 1960s. In particular, this sort of thing could easily be had for the very popular Ford Mustang. I was a member of an online Plymouth Valiant group so I posted a question about dealing with the sag and the availability of parts. Bingo! Before long a member responded with information on a company in Rhode Island offering exactly what I was looking for. Replacements for most if not all frame members were available along with what I needed, subframe connectors. In essence, the Valiant has front and rear subframes held together by the body. The subframe connectors are exactly what they sound like, heavy steel tubes that can be welded to the subframes to connect them. There are claims that Chrysler engineers intended for convertibles to have similar parts from the factory but were overruled by accountants. Maybe true; maybe not.

Of course, I needed someone to install the connectors so I turned to, as you may have predicted, the friend of a friend. My search for advice and parts ran into December of 2011 which is when I started trying to schedule the installation. The car went into the shop in the latter part of February. It came out on May 17. In addition to removing the sag and installing the connectors, the master brake cylinder and some questionable brake lines were replaced. While three months is hardly explained by the amount of work done, I didn't really mind and even encouraged a "no rush" approach.

About a month after I got the car back, I took it on a sort of trial run. The 2012 Lincoln Highway Association National Conference was in Canton, Ohio, in June. Canton is about 200 straight-line miles from my home. Actual driving miles would be a little more but a round trip in the 500 mile range seemed likely and what better road trip to initiate a car purchased to drive the Lincoln Highway than one centered around the year's biggest Lincoln Highway event. The trip spanned seven days but for three of them the car sat idle in a parking garage. Over days one and two, I drove at a very leisurely pace to a classic motel on the east side of Canton. On the third, I drove the last fifty or so miles to Niles, Ohio, to join a preconference tour that ended up in Canton. I drove sort of directly home on the trip's seventh day after the conference ended. The car performed admirably and even drew a few nice comments from other conference attendees. My confidence that the old Valiant might actually see me through the centennial drive was increased significantly.

So, with a year to go before the big trip and apparently no major mechanical projects required, I could think about what might be considered cosmetic improvements. I drove the car a bit through the summer then took it back to the fellow who had replaced the top to get the seats recovered and the carpet replaced. There was still no danger of mistaking my Valiant for a show car but it wasn't looking too bad.

I had been involved in replacing the heater core when a slot became available for doing the seats and carpet so I finished that up during the winter. I also upgraded the ignition.

By this time, my own plans had merged with Lincoln Highway Association plans and I had signed on to be part of an organized tour for at least part of the drive over the highway. In an email exchange with one of the organizers of the tour, I remarked on the questionable reliability of the old car. He responded that, if I just took along "a set of points and condenser, and possibly a spare fuel pump" I'd probably have one of the more reliable cars in the whole group. I took that to heart and then a bit farther.

Three areas, brakes, fuel delivery, and ignition, seem to stand out when considering the basic ways in which modern cars have been improved over their predecessors. Replacing drum brakes with disks is a known science and I had considered it; same with replacing the carburetor with fuel injection. Though I certainly don't question their value, both are fairly costly and complicated. By comparison, replacing mechanical points with solid state technology is rather inexpensive and simple. At least it should be.

I started laying in some spare parts for the trip. I bought a couple of belts, hoses, and, as advised, a fuel pump. Then, instead of spare points, I bought a Pertronix solid state ignition kit. Installing it was a little more involved than changing points but not horribly so. I made the swap myself and was very pleased and a little surprised when the car started right up when I was done. I was also surprised but not at all pleased to find the car running pretty rough when I backed it out of the garage. It made it around the block but it sure didn't like being fed much gas or being put under much load.

The symptoms seemed just like those I associated with incorrect timing. The kit I had installed went inside the distributor. The distributor base had not been moved nor, as far as I knew, had anything else related to timing. That online group that had helped with the sagging unibody had helped even more in selecting the ignition kit. I went back to them with my latest problem and soon learned that the timing of the Pertronix probably was different than the mechanical setup and retiming the car was definitely in order. It was an explanation that I was happy with and I set out to correct the timing.

13

I found the timing notch on the pulley and slathered it with Wite-Out. I cleaned off the bracket with the timing mark on it and pointed the timing light right at it. I saw nothing. I slathered and maneuvered but I simply could not see any white in the strobe of the timing light. I had never been very good at this and I decided my aging eyes were to blame. There were already a few things I planned on having a pro tend to before the trip so I just added timing to the list.

The start date for that organized tour was June 22. It was mid-April when I gave up on ever getting the timing right myself and set out to arrange some professional help. The last work done on the car, other than the interior, had been the installing the frame connectors and replacing the master cylinder. Returning the car to where that had been done seemed to make sense. Calls to the two telephone numbers I had got no response. Knowing the business was in the process of moving, I made multiple calls and left messages. I was about to move on when I decided to try an email contact. That got an answer which told me to call one of the numbers I had been calling on Monday. I called on Monday, this time the call was answered, and I was told to bring the car up before the end of the week so they could start work on the following week.

I dropped the car off on Friday and, since the shop owner wasn't there at the time, followed up with an email identifying the work I had in mind. I suggested and expected a call on Monday but did not get one until a week later. It didn't take long to realize that the email had not been seen. It was found and discussed and I thought things might be moving ahead. The feeling was even reinforced by another call on some detail later that same day. It was the last call I ever got from the shop owner.

After more than a week of no contact, I tried calling. Several calls, both before and after Memorial Day weekend went unanswered and the messages left went without responses. I finally made a visit on the following Wednesday. The owner was again absent. Some work had been done on the car but not much. In particular, the timing question had not been addressed. I made the two employees I spoke with aware of my disappointment and headed off to meet a friend and cool down. On Friday I got a call from an employee, or maybe just a friend, who I'd had no contact with previously, to tell me that they had done all they could do and that I should pick up the poorly running car. It's hard for me to imagine a worse way for a business to inform a customer of their failure. Yes, the owner was there. No, he couldn't talk just then. Yes, he would call me back shortly.

Not surprisingly, that did not happen. I waited over an hour before calling back. The owner did come to the phone this time and explained that there were some serious problems with the car. There were "two dead cylinders" and any further progress would involve "digging into the engine". I did not really question the diagnosis. As much as I had jerked the timing around, I thought it possible that I had burned some valves or damaged something else. I was, however, livid that it had taken four weeks to determine this.

Before I picked up the car I arranged to take it to the garage that had done the alignment and replaced the main seal. I wasn't looking for a different diagnosis as much as for a more detailed diagnosis. The four weeks in the shop combined with the time spent making contact meant that there was less than three weeks remaining before departure. I told myself that, in the right hands, a lot could be accomplished in three weeks but I also mentally prepared myself to be driving the Lincoln Highway in my Subaru.

A day and a half after moving the car, I learned that two plug wires were found reversed. The car was now running fine. Two plug wires!?! Reversed?!? I had never intentionally unplugged any plug wire while installing the electronic ignition but the distributor cap had certainly been off and it's easy for me to believe that wires had popped out and been incorrectly replaced at that end. I am, of course embarrassed that I caused the problem then failed to detect it. I'd be a lot more embarrassed if I was a professional mechanic with four weeks to suss things out.

It took a little longer to get everything done that I wanted but I picked up the smooth running Valiant with days to spare. California here we come. But first New York.

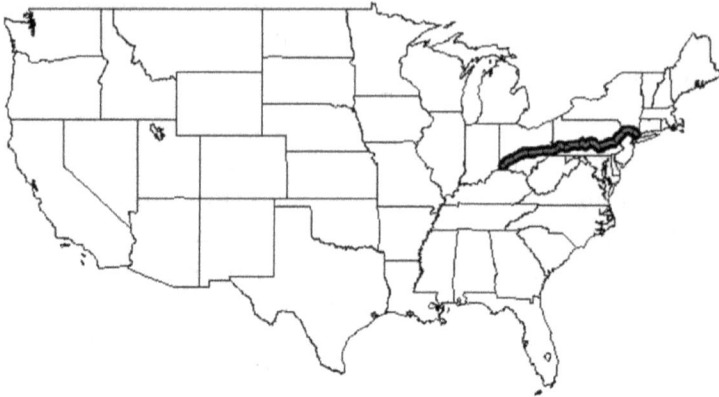

4 TO ROLL

I hinted that I had aligned my own plans with those of the Lincoln Highway Association. The current Association is the second. It was formed in 1992. The original was incorporated on July 1, 1913, and that's the date the party planners focused on.

As long as I've been paying attention, the annual Lincoln Highway Association conference has taken place toward the end of June. It would not take too much shifting to align it with that anniversary date. As I understand it, Kearney, Nebraska, was selected for the 2013 conference fairly early in the planning sequence. Kearney's location near the center of the highway made it a somewhat natural choice for this landmark year. Of course, something akin to that 2003 caravan should happen during the centennial year and maybe it could also be aligned with the anniversary date somehow. Past LHA President Bob Lichty is credited with the idea of having two caravans meet in Kearney. His wife, Rosemary Rubin, is credited with making it happen.

The actual conference, with lectures, bus tours, and other events, would be for members only. With the big anniversary bringing more attention to the Lincoln Highway, adding something more open seemed like a good idea. In the end, a trio of coordinated events was scheduled. First, the two caravans would meet in Kearney and participate in a parade on the day before the LHA anniversary. A festival-like birthday party would fill the anniversary day itself and the three day conference would follow. The parade and birthday party were public affairs in which the city of Kearney played a major role in planning and executing.

I recall getting a few inklings of the "two caravan" approach at the 2008 Ohio Lincoln Highway League annual meeting. In 2010, I attended my first national Lincoln Highway Association conference and picked up another inkling or two. By the 2011 conference, plans were really coming together and the whole Kearney parade and party thing was being presented and promoted. I had my ride, the 1963 Valiant, in hand and was eager to learn as much as I could about the pre-parade caravans. Details were still sparse but the overall plan was firming up. With the arrival parade set for June 30, one day in advance of the anniversary, the cars would have to be in or very near Kearney on the 29th. A rough schedule with potential overnight stops had been worked out for the two caravans. Some of those stops would change as the plan was refined over the next two years but the start points and dates would not. The east group, which I hoped to be part of, would depart from New York City on June 22. The west group would leave San Francisco one day later on June 23. According to some, the difference came from less congestion and longer uninterrupted drives in the west. Others claimed that westerners just drive faster.

I guess it was about the time of the 2011 conference that I picked up on the fact that the organizers were using the word "tour" rather than "caravan" when referring to the groups of cars. They felt that "caravan" conjured up images of long lines of automobiles travelling nose to tail through towns and country and that was not at all what was intended. What was intended was that the cars would travel in small groups with departures and arrivals spread throughout some window of time. Nose to tail lines of more than just a few cars not only cause problems for everyone else, they are darned hard to maintain and dangerous, too. So the groups of cars heading to the doings in Kearney would be on tours. In practice, the word came to be used not only for what the groups were doing but for the groups themselves. I've used "caravan" up to this point because I thought that "tour" required some sort of explanation and I did not find a place to slip it in until now. I will henceforth get with the program and talk no more of caravans.

The previous chapter told of what was going on in preparing the car for the big trip. For its owner, there was little preparation at all until the last few weeks. Normally, for a trip of this length, I would have been plotting a route, guessing at overnight stops, and, if I anticipated difficulty or there was a particular place I wanted to stay, making reservations. For this trip, I had people for that.

I have already explained that Rosemary Rubin was the person "making it happen". "It" included stops for meals, roadside attractions, and sleeping. Discounts had been arranged with Holiday Inn and it was the official hotel of the tours. By simply supplying Rosemary with a credit card number, I had a reserved place to sleep each night.

The route was also taken care of. A complete online map of the Lincoln Highway with all its alignments had debuted during the 2012 national conference in Canton. The foundation was Google Maps. The interactive map included not only all the various alignments but roadside attractions and historical notes as well. Paul Gilger was chairman of the committee that produced this and Paul would also be the guide for the western centennial tour. Eastern tour guide duties were handled by Jim Peters. Using the same technology as the overall map, a map of the tour route was produced. In addition, both guides produced turn by turn instructions that became available a couple of months before the launch date. When that happened, I tackled my own bit of preparation.

I typically travel alone and rely on a GPS receiver to keep me on track if there is a track I want to be kept on. Over the course of many trips I have worked out a procedure for getting a route plotted and loaded into the unit so that it can be fed back to me, visually as well as by voice, as I drive it. I had been spared the task of determining the route but I still needed to plot and download it. It is fairly tedious and time consuming but the few hours spent on each day's route is more than paid back in getting through unfamiliar intersections by my lonesome. I also printed out the instructions for backup and for use by the navigator during the early part of the trip when I would not be by my lonesome.

John a close friend, had long been penciled in as a co-traveler. In February, this became official and John registered for the NYC to Kearney tour. He would probably fly home from somewhere near

Kearney but that was not cast in concrete. Nor was it initially decided whether he would ride with me to New York or fly. Those were mere details.

At the end of the last chapter, the car was proclaimed ready. At roughly the same time, so were the GPS files. Allowing myself three days to reach Secaucus, New Jersey, where the pre-launch dinner was being held, I headed east on US 22 on Wednesday morning. John had decided to maximize time at work by flying to Newark but, since my route went right by his office, I made a stop just in case a last minute break through would let him climb aboard a little early. No such luck.

I drove on through Ohio and West Virginia and into Pennsylvania. I spent the first night near Pittsburgh and the second between Harrisburg and Allentown. The weather was beautiful, the Valiant was running fine, and I arrived in Secausus on Friday afternoon with renewed confidence. Several years of planning and waiting were about to end.

Wednesday lunch stop at Kim's Classic Diner, Sabina, OH

Friday afternoon crossing Pulaski Skyway to Jersey City, NJ

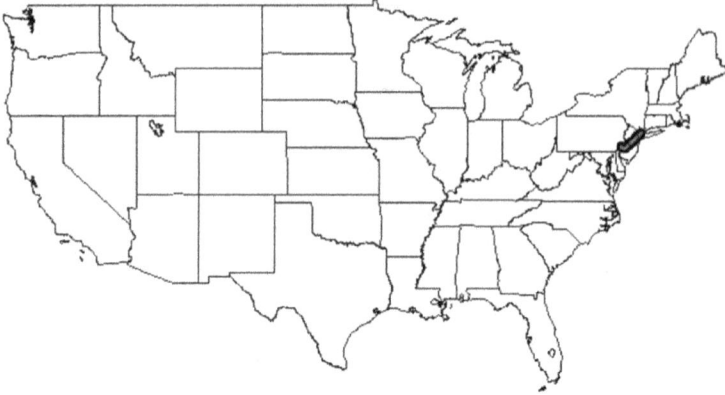

5 WE'RE OFF

I picked up John at the airport as planned then scooted back to the hotel. We arrived at the kick-off dinner a little later than most so did an eat and register instead of the more common register and eat. Announcements followed the meal

Jim Peters at the kickoff dinner

and there were a few discussions before everyone headed off to rest up for an early start. I paid the Valiant a visit before bedding down.

All of the tour cars were safe inside the fence around the valet parking area where the Valiant seemed a little outclassed among Packards and Lincolns some of which were many years its senior. A problem had been discovered on the drive from the airport and I hoped I could do something about it. While sitting in traffic, a neighboring driver called out that our brake lights were not working. We soon pulled into a gas station to top up and poked and pulled stuff in the brake light area before moving on. Although we had no luck getting the lights to work, we did have some absolutely wonderful luck in making it to the hotel without getting rear-ended.

John and I suspected the brake pedal switch. My after dinner visit to the car was to see if I might be able to free a stuck switch or at least prove the theory and get a feel for how to replace it. In the process, I discovered that the left taillight was simply not lighting at all. I removed the bulb and studied it closely then replaced it and reseated the socket with appropriate firmness

Tour cars on the eve of launch

and twisting of both the socket and my jaw. The taillight was healed and so too were the brake lights. It was magical and a great relief.

The Lincoln Highway was never actually signed in the state of New York but Times Square is universally accepted as its eastern terminus. That is where the tour part of this expedition would officially start. Even with the chance of being rear-ended in Times Square slightly reduced by having working brake lights, my night was not particularly restful and I was up way too early. Driving the Valiant through Manhattan was something that I looked forward to and absolutely dreaded in roughly equal measure. I dislike driving in Atlanta or Chicago, I loathe driving in Los Angeles or Washington, and there are many more cities that I am not at all fond of driving in, but New York City is special. I fear it. It's illogical, I know. Nothing bad has ever happened to me there. I've seen crazier drivers in Los Angeles and worse gridlock in Chicago but New York City intimidates me like no other American city. I drove through Times Square in 2008 to begin a partial Lincoln Highway drive and there was never a question of me doing it this time but I would sure be glad when it was over.

There were three of us in the Valiant for the drive into the city. A week or so before, LHA president Kay Shelton had sent me a note asking if I would be driving into Manhattan. If, so, could she hitch a ride. Of course, I replied but rechecked in the morning to see if she knew what she was getting herself into. Not everyone with near waist length hair wants to go running around in a fifty year old top down convertible. She knew and, while

Into Manhattan through the Lincoln Tunnel
(photo by John Nawrocki)

gentleman John climbed into the back seat, Kay pulled her hair into a long pony tail and we hit the road.

The Times Square passage might not have been the tour's finest moment but we did it. Briefly stopping a lane of traffic as had been done in 2003 was never part of the plan. The LHA asked; NYC said no. Then a last minute unavoidable cancelation took away the volunteer who would have snapped a photo of each car as it passed through 42nd & Broadway. Twenty some cars made the drive and each was essentially on its own. At one extreme were people who had recently cased the place and, with advance planning, managed to get a picture of their car with an identifiable background. At the other end were those making wrong turns, multiple unsure passes, and other faux pas. I believe that everyone wanting to drive by the terminus eventually did so but I cannot swear to that. We were somewhere in between. We made no wrong turns but neither did we get any photographic evidence of our visit to the key intersection. It would certainly have been possible to loop back and try again had the Manhattan-phobic driver (me) not been so intent on escape. John did get a shot of our passage through the Lincoln Tunnel and we have each other as witnesses.

A hundred years ago, driving the Lincoln Highway from that Times Square terminus meant taking the 42nd Street ferry across the Hudson River to Weehawken, New Jersey. A ferry still runs to

Weehawken but carries only passengers. Tour participants choosing not to enter Manhattan would start at Weehawken. Those of us who started at Times Square would connect with them there after entering and exiting New York via the Lincoln Tunnel which, despite its name, was never part of the Lincoln Highway.

The drive through Times Square was Kay's second adventure of the weekend and she was just getting started. After flying into La Guardia Friday evening, she got hooked up with a limo driver who seemed to have no idea where he was going and gave Kay an unwanted tour of a sizable chunk of New York before finally getting her to Secaucus, New Jersey, a couple of hours late. Another limo, hopefully with a more astute driver, would pick her up at Weehawken and return her to the airport for a flight to San Francisco for the launch of the western tour on Sunday. Then it was a flight back to Chicago for a few days work before reconnecting with the east tour on our pass through Joliet, Illinois, on Thursday. Whew!

At Weehawken with New York City in background

Though all tour participates passed through the Weehawken landing area, there was no coordinated launch. John and I took some pictures, got Kay to the top of the hill to meet the limo, then moved on with others.

We were moving away from the dreaded Manhattan but not from congestion. In addition to New York City, Philadelphia had to be endured today and, though they were the biggest, those two were certainly not the only cities we passed through. Jersey City and Trenton come to mind and I know there were others. They run together with nothing other than a sign or a line on a map to separate them.

I had driven this section before and did not expect to see anything new but I did and that, plus the built-in excitement of starting a cross country trip, somewhat balanced my distaste for the non-stop high-rise buildings and congested streets. In 2008, I had not stopped at the James Earle Fraser statue of Lincoln in Jersey City. The whole group did so today even though it was not scheduled. I believe that at this point, much of the tour was trying to behave like a caravan with synchronized stops and starts.

Tour cars in Jersey City, NJ

Lincoln the Mystic, **Jersey City, NJ**

There was a scheduled stop at the Edison Museum in Menlo Park. I had stopped here in 2008 but the museum had not been open then so I again got to see something new today. Plus there was the promise of even better things

Edison Memorial Tower at Menlo Park

to come. In 2008, the Edison Memorial Tower, topped by a giant light bulb, had been fenced off to prevent people being next to it when another chunk fell off. It was in pretty bad shape. Today it was fenced off to guard the major renovation taking place.

Lunch was at the east edge of Princeton in a pleasant little park by the Delaware and Raritan Canal. Here we could enjoy the provided bag lunch at a picnic table by the canal and relax a bit. There were some historic displays, both inside and outside of the park buildings, and even a few old cars to look at. The stop was well timed to recharge for Trenton and Philadelphia which were just ahead.

Delaware and Raritan Canal near Trenton, NJ

In general, the only daily event with a specific time was dinner. There was always a lunch break and usually morning and afternoon breaks but these were scheduled over a short window of time so that people could roll through at their convenience. The morning and afternoon stops often included refreshments. They always included restrooms.

There was no official afternoon stop on that first day but the driving instructions allowed plenty of time for checking out Philadelphia attractions like Independence Hall and the Liberty Bell. John and I skipped any sightseeing stops but a

Downtown Philadelphia
(Photo by John Nawrocki)

missed turn and some construction soon has us ad libbing the route just a bit. At some point a couple of fellows on the opposite side of the street called out to us but we were already past. Something about them, now forgotten, made us circle back. The two had crossed the street by the time we got back and we stopped beside where they waited. One handed John a piece of paper which turned out to be a copy of a citation, signed by Philadelphia's mayor, recognizing the Lincoln Highway's Centennial. Spot checking has not yet turned up anyone else who received a copy.

The day's destination was not far from Philadelphia and really not all that far from where we started. In ten plus hours, we had covered just about 125 miles of Lincoln Highway and were less than 100 crow miles from Times Square. But they were busy miles and important miles and it felt good to have taken that first step in the journey west.

City Of Philadelphia
Michael A. Nutter, Mayor

CITATION

Philadelphia is home to many historical sites, not only for the City, but for the entire nation as well. Philadelphia has made the preservation of historical sites a priority so future generations will have the opportunity to see where they came from and where the City began.

One of Philadelphia's many connections to history is the trolley on Lancaster Avenue in West Philadelphia - the very last active trolley on Lincoln Highway. Lincoln Highway is celebrating its 100th anniversary this year by holding a special tour. The Lincoln Highway 100th Anniversary Tour will start simultaneously in Times Square, New York and in the urban centers of San Francisco, California, and eventually meeting in Kearney, Nebraska.

Travelers participating in the tour have the unique opportunity to see antique and modern cars, trucks, and motorcycles commemorating the monumental anniversary of this historic highway. Throughout the tour, travelers will be able to witness the breathtaking scenery that Philadelphia and our suburbs, as well as other locations throughout the country, have to offer.

Lincoln Highway was one of the first transcontinental highways in the United States that was built for automobiles. Created in 1913, the Lincoln Highway was also America's first national memorial for President Abraham Lincoln. With the existence of the Lincoln Highway came monumental prosperity in the hundreds of cities, towns, and villages that it passed through.

It is fitting and appropriate, therefore, that the City of Philadelphia officially recognize with this Citation

THE LINCOLN HIGHWAY 100TH ANNIVERSARY TOUR

for preserving and honoring the significance of the Lincoln Highway, not only to Philadelphia but to the country as well.

Michael A. Nutter
Mayor

June 22, 2013

LHA Centennial Citation from the Mayor of Philadelphia

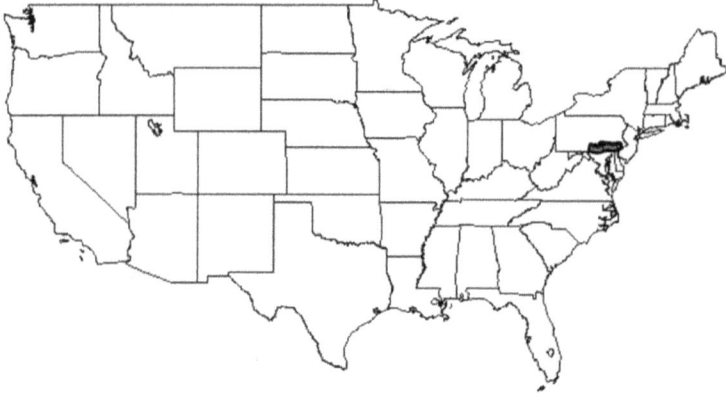

6 A DAY IN THE COUNTRY

The tour's second day began in a much more relaxed manner than had the first. Although all the cars were on the road rather early, there was no fixed departure time and drivers rolled out singly or in small groups pretty much when they felt like it.

Hotel parking lot, Malvern, PA

I could be extra relaxed today not only because that New York City thing was out of the way but because John was doing the driving.

The current US 30 really does follow the route of the original Lincoln Highway through most of Pennsylvania and it is where we spent much but not all of our day. As US 30 approaches Lancaster, it becomes increasingly commercial. I've driven this section more than once so did not feel at all guilty when, following a suggestion in the tour driving instructions, we left US 30 about twenty miles east of

Lancaster to pick up PA 340 for a bit of rural Amish country. This was a significant and welcome change from yesterday's surroundings.

Farm country east of Lancaster, PA

At Lancaster's edge, we rejoined the route of the Lincoln Highway, though not US 30 which bypasses both Lancaster and York, and drove through the historic town. The Susquehanna River is about ten miles beyond Lancaster with the town of York about ten miles beyond that. In 1931, shortly after the mile and a half long Columbia-Wrightsville Bridge was completed over the Susquehanna, red roses

Columbia-Wrightsville Bridge

were planted along the road at the bridge's east end with white ones being planted on the west. Get it? York, Lancaster? War of the Roses? A few red and white roses grow at the appropriate ends of the bridge today – but not many.

When we crossed the Susquehanna, we realized that we would be way early for lunch if we just continued and decided to do some shopping. John's under-padded backside was not well served by the 1960s bench seat. I had no shortage of padding but found the air tight vinyl a bit uncomfortable in the heat. We set off to find some of those beaded automatic-massaging all-day-comfort-giving pads that bus and taxi drivers do endorsements for. There is no surprise, I'm sure, in reading that Sunday morning in Columbia, Pennsylvania, is neither the best place nor time to shop for odd automotive accessories. There were no automotive stores open but we did find a Kmart and picked up a pair of pads that were well below taxi driver quality but a definite improvement over the bare vinyl.

Just east of York and a smidgen off the Lincoln Highway, the Haines Shoe house was a sort of combination morning break and lunch stop. Starting at 11:00, we could get a tour of the house and pick up a box lunch. Gettysburg is just a half-hour or so away and both the early access to and the portability of lunch were for the benefit of those wanting to maximize time at the battlefield. John and I toured the house then ate at a picnic table

Haines Shoe House near York, PA

in the yard before moving on to Gettysburg.

Virginia Memorial at Gettysburg

The 150th anniversary of the first day of the Battle of Gettysburg was just a week and a day away. Anticipating, quite correctly, a large crowd, we devised a plan. Both John and I had visited most of the historic sites before so did not feel a great need to cover them again. On the other hand, there was a new movie and other attractions at the visitors center that would no doubt be interesting if convenient. It wasn't; convenient, that is, which kept us from learning if it was interesting. Our plan was to drive to the visitors center and, if the crowd was not too bad, stop to see the movie. Otherwise, we would just move on. All parking areas even slightly near the visitors center were full and the pathways and roadsides leading to the center were lined with people walking from and to some fairly remote locations. The signed driving tour, which we followed just a tiny bit of, was almost as crowded. With various events planned for the sesquicentennial, the little town almost certainly got even more crowded as the week progressed.

Appalachian Brewing Company, Gettysburg, PA

We cooled off at Appalachian Brewing Company before leaving town then stopped at Mister Ed's Elephant Museum & Candy Emporium. This was my first visit since the big 2010 fire. Although the place is laid out a little differently than it had been, it seems to have completely recovered. I understand that lots of gifts helped replace elephant related items lost to the fire and the museum appears as well populated as before. Plus I believe it is better arranged. Mister Ed has not been here on any of my three or four stops which naturally gives me a reason to return.

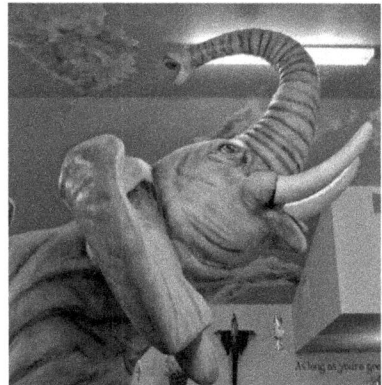

One of Mr Ed's many elephants

At the end of the day we learned of incidents involving the two oldest cars traveling with the eastern tour. One was a 1916 Oldsmobile owned by a Vermont couple. Their plan was to trailer the car to the staging area near Kearney then drive it in the parade. They would follow the full tour route and display the car at the overnight stops where practical. I saw it in the motel parking lot in Malvern but failed to get a photograph. Today a truck struck the trailer destroying it and the gorgeous Oldsmobile inside. The tow vehicle and its occupants were unhurt and the truck driver's injuries were, reportedly, minor. The owners continued with the tour for a day or two but it quickly became too much and they returned home. Even though it obviously could have been so much worse, the event was still rather unnerving.

The second incident was an engine fire involving a 1918 Dodge Brothers Army Staff Car. The fire left the car disabled but repairable. It was scheduled to leave the tour in Pittsburgh so its outing was cut short by just a day and within a few miles of home. The car had covered the Lincoln Highway west from Gettysburg in 2009 when it participated in the reenactment of the 1919 Motor Transport Corps Convoy. By getting as far as it did on this trip, the Dodge could now consider the Lincoln Highway done.

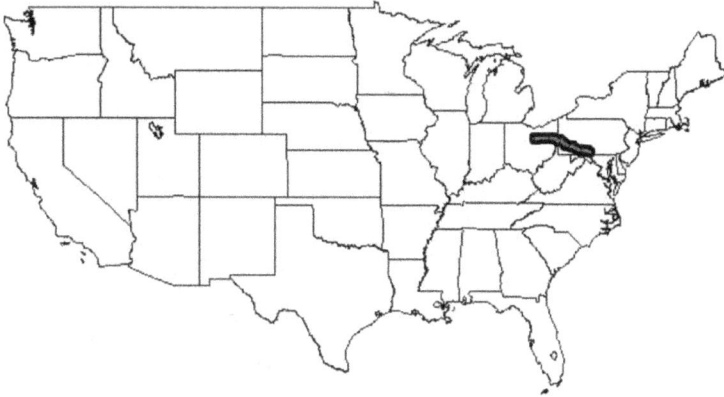

7 PENNYSLVANIA AND BEYOND

Monday's drive took us through one of my favorite Lincoln Highway towns, Bedford, Pennsylvania. The town itself is not especially spectacular and even the things that attract me may not be world beaters individually but the group of roadside attractions clustered around Bedford is, to me, a true microcosm of the Lincoln Highway. Four things in particular support that view. The centerpiece is Dunkel's gas station which the Dunkel

Dunkel's Station in Bedford, PA

family continues to operate just as they have since Dick Dunkel originally opened the place in 1933. A giant coffee pot sits in front of the fairgrounds about a half mile from the station. The big pot was built in 1927 as a lunch stand but saw many different uses over the years. It was abandoned and in pretty bad shape prior to its 2004 restoration. The other two attractions in my set of four are a little west of town. Roughly three and a half miles beyond the Coffee Pot, the eighteenth century Jean Bonnet Tavern still offers overnight accommodations and serves meals. It's where we had lunch. The 1940s Lincoln Motor Court is quite active just a couple miles further on. There is more to Bedford than these but a seventy year old motor court, an eighty year old art deco service station, and an even older bit

John at Bedford, PA, Coffee Pot

of programmatic architecture combined with a two and a half century old road house is a pretty good mix to start with.

John and I added something a little south of Bedford. For the second day in a row, we were going to be much too early for lunch

Bedford Springs Resort

but today, rather than go shopping, we went sightseeing. We turned off of the Lincoln Highway in downtown Bedford and drove a few miles south to Bedford Springs Resort. The luxury resort first opened in 1806, fell into disrepair in the late twentieth century, then was restored and reopened in 2007. It has been visited by a total of ten US presidents starting with James Polk in 1848. It's just a bit off of the Lincoln Highway and certainly worth the short drive for a look-see. Spending the night is probably also worth the price but I wouldn't know about that.

After doing a little exploring of the resort, we returned to the Lincoln, filled the tank at Dunkel's, stopped by the Coffee Pot and Lincoln Motor Court, then headed to the Jean Bonnet Tavern for lunch. Today's lunch came in a bag and some folks moved on down the road with theirs. We took ours to the second floor deck where a small-world moment awaited. As we considered where to sit, a lady sitting alone closed the book she was reading and invited us to join her. This was Rose. She lived nearby and was familiar with our tour and thought we might swap road tales and local information. A pleasant conversation was soon underway. We learned that Rose did quite a bit of trailer camping in her Serro Scotty. I don't know much about camping trailers but I did recognize the name because friends of mine own one. Out of curiosity, I asked and got a quick yes. Of course she knew Pat and Jennifer. Serro Scotty owners are both far flung and close knit.

Lincoln Motor Court,
Manns Choice, PA (July 3, 2008)

Jean Bonnet Tavern,
Bedford, PA (July 3, 2008)

Conversation came to an abrupt halt when someone called out a rain warning. There had not been a hint of rain when we stopped but the sky was now dark and threatening. We ran to the car to put the top up. Rose came along to say goodbye and a reporter asked a few questions as we rolled up windows and watched the clouds. Turns out there was a photographer there, too, and a picture of the soon to be wet Valiant appeared on the front page of the next day's Bedford Gazette.

The Valiant was far from water tight. The new top was solid but rubber seals were ancient or missing. When the rain hit, it was fairly intense for several minutes. We sat in the parking lot as we chased drips with towels and kept gear and paper as dry as possible. Parking during cloudbursts would not always be possible but when it was, it was the preferred action.

The rain did not last terribly long. When it had all but stopped, we moved up the road to a new Bedford attraction. It's not quite clear just when the faux gas station between the Jean Bonnet Tavern and the Lincoln Motor Court first became a roadside attraction. It seems

Ron Miller in front of his mini-museum

Ron Miller restored cars and radios there for quite some time before declaring it a mini-museum. There are some gas pumps in front and other automotive related paraphernalia here and there but the radios are the main draw. A small building is filled with them, some from as long ago as the 1920s. They all work and they all have a story. Ron did all the restoration and is pretty good at telling the stories, too.

Not only is Bedford home to a cluster of manmade attractions, it is in a naturally scenic area. The appropriately named Grand View Point is about fifteen miles west of the city limits. This was where the Ship Hotel, destroyed by fire in 2001, once stood. Even without the hotel, it is a popular stop. A few remnants of the hotel remain but the real attraction is, as it has always been, the view. Advertising for the hotel boasted that you could "See 3 States and 7 Counties" from here. Maryland is a little more than twenty miles away and, since Grand View Point is directly north of Maryland's skinniest part, West Virginia is just about five miles farther. I'm not so sure I can see West Virginia but I can sure see a long way.

Grand View Point

We made two more planned stops before the day ended. The first was at the Flight 93 Memorial a few miles west of Grand View Point and just slightly south of the Lincoln Highway. Flight 93 was the hijacked airliner forced down by courageous passengers on September 11, 2001, before it could reach the target Al-Qaeda terrorists intended. This was my third visit to the site. I was here in November of 2004 and again in May of 2008. About the only thing

Mementos at Flight 93 Memorial

that changed between those two visits was that the volunteers at the site on my first visit had been replaced by National Park Service employees on the second. The permanent Memorial Plaza opened in 2011. A small building, a stone marker, and four sections of chain link fencing had been erected sometime prior to my first visit. The chain link was not a barrier but a panel where visitors left various mementos. Leaving

37

these personal tributes was often an important part of a visit to the memorial and the practice continues to be supported with small shelves in the wall along the long walkway. Items, particularly those needing protection from the elements, are regularly removed, cataloged, and stored. More than 50,000 objects were already in this collection at the time of our visit.

Our second stop of the afternoon was at the Lincoln Highway Experience just west of Ligonier. This was my first visit to the combination museum and Lincoln Highway Heritage Corridor headquarters that was opened near the end of 2011. Then it was on to Pittsburgh and dinner.

Lincoln Highway Experience, Ligonier, PA

I earlier mentioned that I thought about replacing the Valiant's drum brakes with modern disks but decided it was too expensive. In Pittsburgh, I thought about it again. Although Grand View Point is the only one I have described, it is hardly the only grand view in Pennsylvania. The state offers several picturesque summits along the Lincoln Highway. Of course everything that goes up must come down and the ups and downs are often at the rate of 8% or so. John had encountered the first of these yesterday and had used the TorqueFlite's second gear to great advantage on some long down grades. I had done the same earlier in today's drive.

Though Pittsburgh is hardly level, it was the frequent stops on our way to the city's center that really were the brake's worst enemy. For the only time on the entire trip, I could sense just a bit of fade in the old drums. The fade was just a reminder. The brakes did their job and, under normal circumstances, did so admirably though on occasion they did need to be applied with extreme prejudice.

Dinner was at the Heinz History Center. The meal was excellent, we had the run of the entire museum, and there was a short talk by author and historian Brian Butko. The LHA had arranged with Brian to produce a book for the centennial with a copy to be provided to each car participating in the Tour. Plans originally called for the book to be distributed along with other tour goodies at the kick-off dinners. Despite some round the

Brian Butko presentation at Heinz History Center

clock efforts by Brian, that had not happened. The book was at the printers and we should get it on arrival in Kearney or maybe before departure from Kearney or maybe – via the US mail – a little bit later. The part of Brian's talk that referred to the book was sort of a preview of coming attractions. Having supplied some of the book's photos and done some of the proofreading, I knew what those coming attractions were but I still looked forward to the finished product with low resolution images replaced by the real thing. With the tour arrival in Kearney just six days away and a stay there of only a few days, I figured there was a pretty good chance I would first see the book when I picked up my mail at trip's end.

The night was spent on the west edge of Pittsburgh south of the Ohio River. We crossed over in the morning and traced the north bank for several miles before pulling away in the town of Beaver. This also took us away from the hustle and bustle of Pittsburgh's suburbs. Our morning break came at a small park near Ohioville containing little more than restrooms and, on this day only, some media folk. After making use of the former, we chatted with the latter. Only after a videographer had clipped a mic on John and started interviewing him beside the Valiant did I realize that all our cameras, including my phone, were inside the car. This seems to have been freelance work and we do not know of the video showing up anywhere. I could take no photos and those promised by an associate of the videographer have not materialized. Sometimes the fleeting comes before the fame.

The winding road beyond the park took us back to the river and we were soon in Ohio. We again pulled away from the river at

John at the wheel with Monaca-Rochester Bridge in background

East Liverpool and headed northwest to our lunch stop at the Steel Trolley Diner in Lisbon. I've eaten at the diner, a 1956 O'Mahony, before and have visited the town's museums, which we also did today, but I did not know about the Steamer.

Local boosters greeted us as we left the diner and one caught our attention with the name Stanley Steamer. A block or so north of the Lincoln Highway in the heart of Lisbon, Ohio, sits a onetime

1923 Stanley Steamer in Lisbon, OH

Chrysler dealership. Among the many cars in the current owner's collection is a completely functional and sometimes driven 1923 Stanley Steamer. As the owner explains it, more of these cars were destroyed in the garage than were ever involved in highway accidents. Instant response was never the steam car's forte and many a "nudge" resulted in high torque motion a bit later and farther than anticipated.

This is almost home territory. The Lincoln Highway passes through Ohio far north of anyplace I've ever lived but I've traveled the Ohio bits more than any other. We stopped at the historic Spread Eagle Tavern in Hanover and the

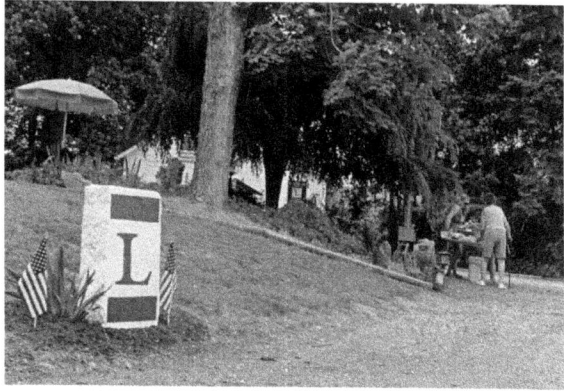

Lemonade stand near Minerva, OH

Lincoln themed IGA in Minerva. West of Minerva, beside the bricks of Baywood Street, we encountered a not for profit lemonade stand. Profit has its place on the Lincoln Highway but it is not even close to being all consuming. A smile and a "Howdy" will likely get you more than a fist full of dollars.

When first laid in the 1920s, the bricks of Baywood Street defined a roadway sixteen feet wide. Several years later, it was widened to eighteen feet by increasing the gap between bricks and adding sand. Separating yourself from modern vehicles and focusing on points where modern signs are hidden can make a drive on this road feel like an eighty year flashback.

Baywood Street near Minerva, OH

In Canton, there was a long and delightful pause at the Canton Classic Car Museum. Since Canton was the site of the 2012 LHA Conference and the Valiant's longest previous outing, this was kind of like a homecoming.

Canton Classic Car Museum

Rain that threatened at the museum in Canton finally caught us as we pulled into the Smucker's Company Store and Café to redeem free ice cream coupons we had been given at the museum. That's where we met Andy.

Andy was driving a 1940 Canadian Lincoln Zephyr. He had planned on joining the tour in Pittsburgh but that had not quite worked out so here he was not quite sure of where the end of day stop was. He asked if he could follow us and we said sure and that's how we learned that the brake lights had had a relapse. "Nothing," Andy told us when we reached the hotel in Mansfield, Ohio. No brake lights at all except for a few flickers as we bounced over rail road tracks or something similar. Then, at the front desk, we learned we were late for dinner.

Andy Harvey's Zephyr at Smucker's

We dashed up the street to find that, while we actually had the right time for dinner and it was the better part of an hour away, there was a pre-dinner program that started an hour before the meal and for which we were obviously late. We learned this from people sitting outside the un-air-conditioned building because it was too hot inside. We stepped inside, decided they were right, and headed back to the

hotel. I naturally felt guilty about missing my own chapter's shindig but my body was most appreciative of the hotel's AC. My guilt was increased by reports of an excellent program and very good meal and decreased by reports of it being

A peek at the pre-dinner program in Mansfield, OH

well attended without me. In the end, I felt somewhat neutral in the guilt department.

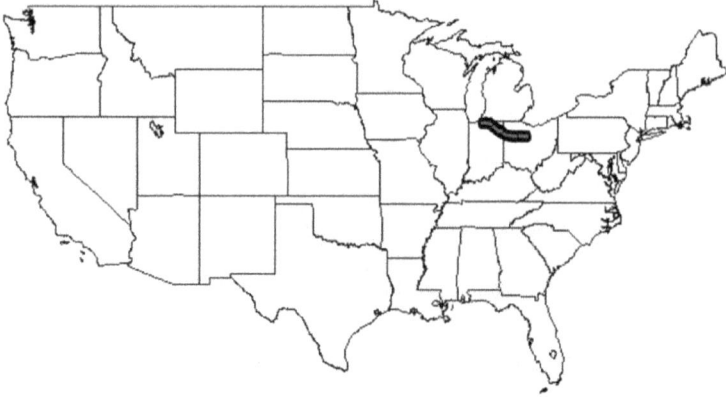

8 FRIENDS AND FAMILY

We now needed to do something about those brake lights. When wiggling wires and twisting sockets and talking with other tour folk did no good, we looked up an auto parts store and headed on over. We bought a volt meter plus some bulbs and wire. I assumed a helpful expression while John poked and prodded with the meter. He found some variations but nothing to account for the outage. For the sake of completeness, we replaced the bulbs which, as expected, did nothing. The next step was to ask the store clerks for a shop recommendation and they responded with absolutely no hesitation. Rex Gilbert Auto Electric was the place to go, they said.

I called and was told that they had a full schedule but would try to work in a look-see. We drove directly there and were pleasantly surprised when a technician immediately stepped outside to check things out. There was more poking and prodding mixed with wiggling and twisting, none of which produced any light. After a fair amount of this, he went inside for a consultation. On return, he ventured the theory that the problem was in the turn signal switch in the steering column. Brakes and turn signals share the same light bulb element with turn signals trumping brakes. If the switch failed in such a way as to be in constant override mode, what we were seeing might be the result.

Finding a replacement in Mansfield seemed unlikely and the odds of getting it quickly installed only slightly better. While a one or two day layover would not necessarily scuttle the trip, it would scuttle a planned lunchtime meeting with friends and family and cause us to miss tour activities for the length of the layover and then some. John and I developed a plan while the technician continued to poke, prod, wiggle, and twist under the dashboard. I would order a replacement and have it sent to my motel in Kearney. I would try to enlist a fellow tour member as an accomplice to follow me and be my rear guard. In Kearney, I could get the switch installed during the conference. Then, just as we were starting to discuss some of our plan's details, the brake lights came on. The technician claimed not to know what he had done. John and I certainly didn't. It was almost certainly temporary but it was something of a reprieve from the sense of emergency and we set off to rejoin the tour. I might still order the suggested switch but I would wait until the end of the day to do it.

Surprisingly, our brake light diversion did not make us all that far behind the tour and we reached Bucyrus before the chase vehicle moved on and while photos were still being taken in front of one of the town's many murals. The Bucyrus Chamber of Commerce had arranged this unique photo op. This was the only time the road's namesake was there to greet us but many Lincoln Highway towns took advantage of the centennial tour to draw a little attention to themselves. It was nice to see towns take pride in their

Mr Lincoln (Gerald Payn) greets us in Bucyrus, OH
(photo by John Peters)

place on the historic road and this might even have been the first time that some residents of Bucyrus and other towns even heard of the Lincoln Highway let alone realized they were part of it. Good news all the way around.

Though I do not doubt that there are a few residents of Lincoln Highway towns who know nothing of the highway that directly connects them to both coasts, it is certainly a very small percentage. Ohio has a history of marking the Lincoln

Lincoln Highway pillars on US 30 overpass at I-75

Highway and often used rather substantial brick pillars to do it. Many of those pillars remain, some that were lost have been replaced, and a few have even been erected in new locations. While the road itself bears little resemblance to the Lincoln Highway of yore, markers on US 30's I-75 overpass invoke those old style pillars. It's the sort of thing that makes it tougher and tougher to remain completely unaware of the historic road.

The day's lunch stop was about a hundred miles beyond Bucyrus and arriving more or less on time was fairly important as we were meeting people there. That meant we skipped the morning's planned break and any other stops we might otherwise have made. From a personal perspective, this was OK since this is my home state and I've driven this section of the Highway several times. However, from

Balyeat's, Van Wert, OH (May 11, 2013)

the perspective of this book, it's not so OK. It means I have no excuse to talk about Upper Sandusky (which has a segment of brick Lincoln Highway), Beaverdam (where the Lincoln and Dixie Highways ran on top of each other for several blocks), or Delphos (where the Miami-Erie Canal and Lincoln Highway once crossed) so I won't. Since we did not eat there, maybe I shouldn't mention Balyeat's Coffee Shop either but we did eat in Van Wert and it just would not seem right to mention the city without also mentioning its oldest (1924) and best known eatery and including a picture from the last time I did eat there.

The plan had been to serve lunch picnic style in a park but the threat of rain prompted a move inside a nearby church. A cousin lives in Van Wert and a long time friend lives a few miles to the west. Both planned to meet us at the park. We spotted Dale, a friend since grade school, as we reached the park. We were directed to a parking spot across from the church where Dale met us. The three of us headed on in where cousin Tammy and her husband, Gary, soon joined us. The rain still threatened but stayed away as the five of us posed, chatted, and walked around the park.

John, Dale, Tammy, and Gary in Van Wert, OH

When Gary and Tammy headed off to another commitment, John and I headed west and Dale, that being the direction of home, followed. We split in Fort Wayne but not before a parking lot meeting with Dale's wife, Marsha. As he followed the Valiant, Dale noted that the driver's side brake light was dimmer than the other. This was the same light that had been out in New Jersey and had been receiving almost all of our attention. During our parking lot farewells, Dale wedged a wire into the light sockets to improve grounding. Doing much the same thing when the light was completely out had not brought it back to life but it seems to have helped this time. Somehow the mixture of amateur and professional poking, probing, wiggling, twisting, and wedging kept the lights working from then on. I don't know why and your guess is at least as good as mine.

What could have been the end of the trip occurred barely an hour later. About two miles south of Kimmell, on a smooth and quiet stretch of two-lane, I nodded off and the Valiant's right tires dropped off of the pavement. I was instantly awake, of course, and quickly, perhaps too quickly, pulled the car back on track. One right side wheel cover took off when the tires left the pavement and the other detached itself when I pulled off into some grass to go look for the first one. At fifty miles per hour, bad things could have happened when the tires left the pavement or when I jerked them back on. They did not.

We drove back along the road looking for the wheel cover then parked and went looking for it on foot. We found it some distance from the road at the edge of a corn field. Both covers went into the back seat where they would stay until parade time in Kearney. Half an hour later, the rain finally arrived and we closed the car as best we could. A few minutes more and we pulled under a gas station canopy to fill the tank and dodge some rain. We drove through Goshen as the deluge subsided and joked about the bullet proof police pillbox by the courthouse. What we did not do was talk about how much today's near disaster reminded us of another one in another red convertible.

In 1999, John and I were on Route 66 in Arizona. I was driving. I started to pull over at the ruins of an old gas station then changed my mind and my abrupt course change caused the Corvette to fishtail. It came back from one slide but ran out of pavement in the other direction. There was no cornfield beside that Arizona two-lane, just a rocky drop off of several feet. We could have rolled but didn't. We had been lucky in Arizona and again in Indiana but we didn't talk about the similarities or the luck or how close we'd come to real disaster. No need to, I suppose. No need to now, either. The incident in Indiana was a significant event in the trip and needed to be included but is not fun to dwell on. I will now move along.

On the road, moving along meant driving to dinner at the National Studebaker Museum in South Bend, Indiana. I had been to the museum more than once but eating there was a whole different – and very cool -- deal. As had been the case at the Heinz History Center in Pittsburgh, dinner included access to the entire museum and we happily took advantage of that.

Dinner at Studebaker Museum

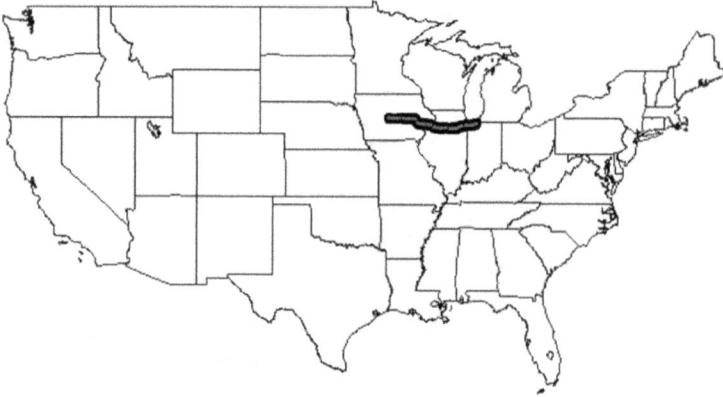

9 ALONE AGAIN (NATURALLY)

I was now travelling solo and the title of Gilbert O'Sullivan's 1972 hit song seemed to fit. Barring a breakdown and an early end to my own trip, it had been all but certain that John would head home before me. Deciding the where and when of his departure, however, was something always left for another day. One scenario had him doing all of the official Centennial Tour and maybe even staying for the parade in Kearney on Sunday then jetting back in time to start the work week on Monday. As attractive as the parade might be, reaching Ohio in less than a day from a place without a major airport was an obvious challenge and heading home from some bigger and more easterly city was more realistic. Maybe a dip down to Omaha or De Moines on Saturday or a similar small detour to Quad City International on Friday. Then, during one of the daily calls home, an alternate plan emerged.

Sherry, John's wife, would drive to meet him and they would have their own little road trip. That was a great idea but the question now became just how little that road trip would be. Omaha and De Moines were automatically ruled out as too far but what about Clinton, Iowa, or Rochelle, Illinois. In the end I think Chicago became the deciding boundary and they settled on South Bend. I was sure sorry to leave John behind but glad that he was able to work in five days on the road. The two of them enjoyed a night out in South Bend then drove home on Friday.

Even the word "naturally" in the song and chapter title fits since I typically travel by myself. But now I had to get re-acclimated. During that time with John in the car, I'd gotten used to sharing opinions on interpreting directions and having help reading signs and snapping drive by photos. I'm quite certain that I pointed out things I passed to the empty seat and asked a few questions aloud the first day and probably the second one, too.

Once outside of South Bend, I drove through pleasant countryside and some nice small towns. The time spent getting the route into the GPS unit was now paying off. It wasn't perfect but it was close and generally kept me on route. Of course,

John Wood grist mill near Merrillville, IN

when the GPS instructions seemed a little confusing, there was now no one to ask for help though, as already confessed, I sometimes asked anyway.

About half way between Valparaiso and Merrillville, we stopped at the restored John Wood Mill for our morning break. The three story brick building was erected in 1876 to replace the original wooden one built in 1838. We passed the site of the

Ideal Section marker (March 29, 2009)

Lincoln Highway's Ideal Section a dozen or so miles later but, while there is a stone marker and bench, traffic makes it tough to visit or photograph and all vestiges of the futuristic – in 1921 – Ideal Section are buried beneath the current US 30. I did not even attempt to stop there today but I do have a photo from an earlier and much colder stop.

The Joliet Area Historical Museum was the day's lunch stop and was also where LHA President Kay Shelton rejoined the tour after hopping from coast to coast to get things started. Between South Bend and Joliet, the Lincoln Highway avoids Chicago by slipping around the city's south side. By the time Joliet is reached, the bulk of Chicago has been passed and the road can start turning northward. It follows a gentle arc to Geneva then makes a sharp turn to head west.

That turn has always been significant. In *The Lincoln Highway: Main Street across America*, Drake Hokanson referred to Chicago as an "…intermission between the first and second acts of a three-act play…" for those traveling from the east coast. What Victor Eubank wrote in 1912, "We were motorists as far west as Chicago. Then we became pioneers." is often quoted to illustrate what early long distance automobilists faced. Things have changed in the intervening century. You no longer need ropes and pulleys and shovels to drive west of Chicago but the road really does start feeling different here. For me, since this is only my second time driving this part of the Lincoln Highway, some of that feeling no doubt comes from unfamiliarity; from the simple fact that the road and some of the stuff beside it are still new to me and still seem fresh. That is not the only reason, however. Most of the big cities really have been passed. San Francisco is out there, of course, and Salt Lake City but they are a long way off and the spaces between them and all the other smaller cities are not entirely filled with four-lane highways, strip malls, and chain restaurants. There are certainly plenty of those things west of Chicago and there are plenty of exceptions to the east but my gut feel is that the ratio really starts shifting about now.

Though the details had yet to be worked out, it had always been my intention to connect with a friend who lives not far from Chicago. At lunch, I learned that meeting up with another friend was also a possibility. Here's the mix. I had exchanged a few emails with Don, a road tripping friend who I've met numerous times, and we had loose plans to meet in Dekalb where he and his wife had gone to college. Cort, who I had met once, and Mike, who I'd had plenty of online conversations with but had only just met on the tour, were planning on meeting for the first time in Geneva. Cort and Mike knew of each other through their shared attraction for big Chevys, especially Monte Carlos. As confusing as that might seem in print, I assure you that it was even more so in real-time.

Using phone calls, a few text messages, and at least one Facebook exchange, we pulled together a Dekalb rendezvous. Cort drove his 1989 Caprice Classic to Geneva where Mike met him in his 1972 Monte Carlo. I met Don in Dekalb and followed him to Fatty's Pub & Grill at which time he provided final approach instructions to the others via phone. And that's how Cort, Mike, Mike's girlfriend Sharon, Don, and I all had

Cort, Sharon, Mike, and Don in Dekalb, IL

Cajun Fried Potato Salad. Pretty good stuff.

The overnight stop was in Rochelle, Illinois, with dinner, hobo stew, a few miles beyond just outside of Franklin Grove. Lincoln Highway Association Headquarters are in Franklin Grove so I worked in a stop to say hello to Lynn who runs the place. I enjoyed the company and the local cars but I skipped the stew. The potato salad might have had a little to do with it but it was mostly my lack of love for stew in general.

There is a visitor's center inside a nicely restored Standard Oil station in Rochelle that makes a good photo op and what has to be one of the most photographed cars on the Lincoln Highway sits just a few miles beyond the city limits. I'm sure that many, perhaps most, of the people pointing cameras at the 1950 Cadillac do not connect it with the Lincoln Highway but many do and it has become something of a must-photograph icon of the road. The car has been there since at least 2007 and there is at least one group devoted to it on the Flickr photo sharing website. Look for "The Old Rusted Cadillac West of Rochelle, Illinois" or just TORCWORI. As I write this, there are about a thousand photographs from more than a hundred members.

The Old Rusted Cadillac West of Rochelle, Illinois

About twenty miles beyond the old Caddy, I passed under the Dixon arch and over the Rock River. I attended my first ever Lincoln Highway Association National Conference in Dixon in 2010. Time sure flies.

Forty miles more and I'm at the Mississippi River. The big windmill that sits beside the Mississippi at Fulton, Illinois, has no connection what

Veterans Memorial Arch, Dixon, IL

so ever with the Lincoln Highway but it's a tough thing to pass up; doubly so on a sunny day. Today was a doubly sunny day. This was our planned morning break and there were guides and greeters at both the mill and the very cool museum. There were refreshments, too, though just walking along the river is mighty refreshing. In four

De Immigrant windmill at Fulton, IL

visits, this has become a favorite stop for me. I like the big mill and the hand built models in the museum are extremely interesting but it is the view of the big river from the well groomed path that I think I like the most.

Iowa is entered by passing under another arch. This one marks the entrance to the city of Clinton on the west bank of the Mississippi River. Plenty of open two-lane awaits just beyond the city.

Entering Clinton, IA (August 16, 2009)

Our lunch stop was in Mount Vernon where, for the only meal of the tour, we were on our own. The town has plenty of good restaurants though none with the capacity to handle the whole group. But finding a meal was certainly not an issue. Walking by the restaurants and picking one you liked was fun and the town looked pretty good with the old cars parked along the street. Cedar Rapids was about a dozen miles away and dessert about a dozen miles beyond that. Local preservationists

Tour cars in Mount Vernon, IA

Youngville Cafe

restored the Youngville gas station and café several years ago but it is

56

only open a few days each week. Today happened to be one of them so I made it inside for the first time and downed a piece of raspberry pie.

A pair of nice surprises awaited in Belle Plaine. Belle Plaine is where George Preston sold gas while he and his station both became Lincoln Highway icons. George became known for the stories he told and the station became known for the signs and license plates that covered it. When George died in 1993, his son Ron became caretaker of the place. Then Ron

George Preston's garage, Belle Plaine, IA

passed away last year and there was an auction. I never met George or Ron but I've been by the station a couple of times and feared that it would be stripped of its signs and personality. Pleasant surprise number one was that the building looked just as it did the last time I saw it in 2010. The area around it was certainly emptier. All those things that some called treasure and others called trash were gone. The treasure presumably sold at the auction. The second surprise was that the station was open. Not open selling gas, it stopped doing that long ago, but open so people could go inside. George's granddaughter Mary was there with her husband greeting visitors and inviting everyone in to look around. There were some other folks there, too. A few older men were sitting beneath the big shade tree. Super friendly fellows who joked as easily with strangers as they did with each other and I have a feeling that those guys knew more than a few stories. I guess that was three pleasant surprises.

I know I should have stuck around and listened to another story or two. I complain about others being in too much of a hurry but I do it myself. There was barely enough time to get to the scheduled dinner stop so I waved goodbye to the men under the tree and moved on. In Tama, I paused just long enough to snap picture of the famous bridge. The bridge with "LINCOLN HIGHWAY" cast into railings might be the best known bridge on the entire highway and I'd bet money that it's the most photographed. I did not really need another picture but I got one anyway. That's the way cameras and icons work.

Lincoln Highway bridge at Tama, IA

Dinner was at Niland's Corner, a place that once had it all. This was a classic one-stop with a restaurant, motel, and service station at the intersection of two major highways. Another named auto trail, the Jefferson Highway, met the Lincoln Highway here and the two traveled together for about fifteen miles until the Jefferson turned south at Ames. Most of the property was donated to the city

Niland's Corner, Colo, IA (June 21, 2010)

of Colo in 1999 and a group now operates the café six days a week and has several motel rooms available for overnight stays. The service station is maintained as an exhibit.

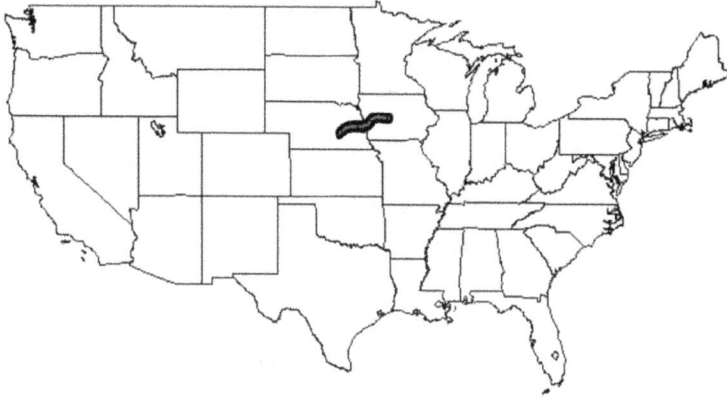

10 KEY EVENTS

After a pulled pork picnic at Niland's, I drove on to the hotel in Ames. In the morning I tried to lock myself out of my car. I doubt that it is actually possible to lock anyone out of a fifty year old convertible but I tried. Thinking that it might at least slow someone down, I do lock the doors at night and I do put the top up. This morning, when I was ready to leave, I walked up to the car, unlocked the trunk, put the normal stuff in it, and closed the lid. Then I walked to the driver's door, reached in my pocket for the keys, and paused. No keys there. I had just unlocked the trunk so I walked to the back of the car thinking I had probably left them in the lock. Nope. Not this time. I now started patting every pocket and visually scouring the ground around the car. The was a drainage grate a few feet away and I got down and peered intently into it. Nothing. I mentally replayed the scene and decided that I must have accidentally dropped (or intentionally placed) the keys inside the trunk while it was open. I had an extra set, of course. They were safe inside my computer bag which was, no surprise here, safe inside the trunk.

So I forced the side windows apart enough to get my hand in and unlocked the door. This maneuver scraped the back of my hand and left a little blood on the glass but I was getting closer to the keys. I climbed into the back seat and pulled part of the vinyl boot loose from where it was glued to the seat back. The bag was naturally at the rear of the trunk but I eventually managed to reach in far enough to snag a bit of strap and pull it toward me. Getting the whole bag out might not have really been possible but I didn't need to do that. I worked the bag around until I found the right zipper then reached in and got the keys.

When I opened the trunk with the spare key and a slightly bloody hand, I was surprised that the other set was not laying in plain sight. I searched under and around the trunk's contents but the keys were nowhere to be found. That was a mystery but not a problem. I looked around the car again then put the top down and drove off.

People in the nearby town of Ogden were preparing for a parade. I seriously considered waiting around for it but it looked like there was still a fair amount of preparing to be done. I made sure I could locate the Ogden Footprints, took a picture, and moved on. Back in 1929, when the main street through town was paved, someone walked across the not quite set concrete.

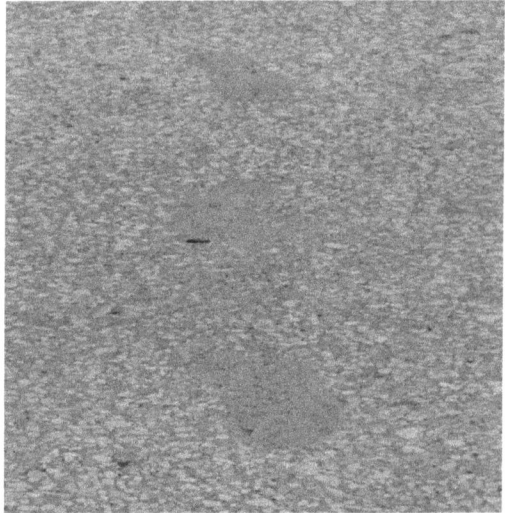

Ogden (Iowa) Footprints

Much of the street has since been covered in asphalt but not the area with the footprints and the prints, though filled and leveled, can still be seen.

The scheduled morning break was in Grand Junction at the Green County

Green County Lincoln Highway Museum, Grand Junction, IA

Lincoln Highway Museum. Iowa's Bob and Joyce Ausberger were instrumental in resurrecting the Lincoln Highway Association in 1992 and it is my understanding that they are also the force behind the museum. Besides the displays and refreshments, quite a few local residents were present at the museum to see the tour cars and many parked their own classic vehicles along the main street.

I also stopped at the monuments erected by Civil War veteran James Moss along the Lincoln Highway near Scranton. In 1926, two years after this stretch of highway was paved, Moss placed the two monuments, with busts of Abraham Lincoln on top, at the edge of his farm as a tribute to Lincoln. Through a series of small steps, the road edges slightly north until,

J E Moss monument near Scranton, IA

about thirty miles west of the Moss markers, the Lincoln Highway reaches its northernmost point and begins angling southwest.

Lunch was in Woodbine, a town proud of its brick Lincoln Highway in a state proud of its loose meat sandwiches. Where I grew up, one of the few sources of drive through fast food was the Maid-

1921 brick pavement in Woodbine, IA

Rite, serving loose meat sandwiches, in Greenville, Ohio. It was an important part of the Saturday night food supply and it was unique, or so I thought. I'm pretty sure it was years after I had moved away from home that I learned there were places called Maid-Rite in other cities. In time I learned that the Maid-Rite name had originated in Iowa and that there was a Greenville-Iowa connection. Maid-Rite was founded in 1926 and was one of the very first restaurants to have franchises. The restaurant in Greenville started out as a franchise in the early 1930s. The distance from Iowa and difficulties of the Great Depression probably figured in the lax enforcement of the franchise agreement and the Greenville operation very quickly became completely independent. Folks in Greenville are intensely proud of their restaurant. Folks in Iowa seem rather proud to be the birthplace of Maid-Rite and quite fond of loose meat sandwiches in general. Though I'll testify that you just can't beat the ones they make in Greenville, I was very pleased to be served a homemade "Maid-Rite" for lunch.

In the afternoon, we stopped at the Gottberg Brew Pub in Columbus, Nebraska, and, yes, beer samples were available. The building housing the brew pub made the stop all the more interesting. Max Gottberg built it in 1920 with decorative

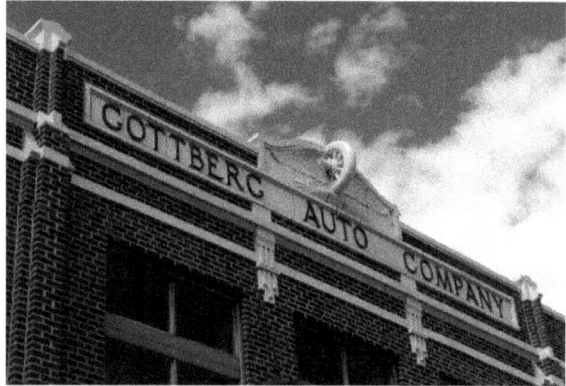

Former Ford dealership in Columbus, NE

touches that left little doubt as to what its purpose was. This was a Ford dealership when the Model T was king. I would get another look when a conference tour stopped here for lunch a few days later.

This next bit is kind of sad and, at the same time, somehow encouraging. Just a few miles west of Columbus, in the town of Duncan, is something called the "Avenue of Trees". Two parallel rows of locust trees mark what was once the Lincoln Highway. The area between the trees is all grass now which may make it even harder to believe that east and west bound travelers used to pass each other between those trees. Following the tour driving instructions, I picked up the original LH alignment and followed a short stretch of gravel into town. I parked and started walking toward the trees to photograph them as a lady approached the Valiant to photograph it.

"Are they behind you?", she asked.

"Who?", I responded and learned that mine was the first car of the centennial tour to enter town. She wondered if the rest of the cars were behind me.

Avenue of Trees in Duncan, NE

With a certain amount of embarrassment, I explained that I was closer to the back of the group than to the front. She looked as if she didn't want to believe me but knew it was the truth. It was fairly late in the day. A couple more tour cars did come into town while I was there but none stopped.

As I finished taking my pictures and started back toward the car, a pickup truck pulled into town and parked. Its driver approached me with a slightly confrontational air. I recognized him as the fellow I'd driven past shortly after leaving Columbus. He had been parked on the shoulder of US 30 attempting to direct tour cars onto an older alignment. The tour was generally following the original 1913 alignment but there were numerous exceptions. That original alignment did indeed turn south where the fellow pointed but I had chosen to stick with the program. So too, apparently, had every other tour car.

The man's name was Mark and his frustration was certainly understandable. He was a Lincoln Highway fan who was highly pleased by the attention the centennial was bringing to the road. The day that the LHA tour passed through should have been a big one. He was responsible for the Lincoln Highway sashes on the trees and some other decorations around town. Mark wasn't exactly angry, although he probably had a right to be, but he was upset. It took awhile for me to become "the guy who stopped at the trees" instead of "one of the guys who just passed him by on the road" but once that happened, I could really enjoy his enthusiasm. At some point Paul, another tour member, joined us and Mark became even happier. He showed us the town's pair of 1928 LH markers and the building that once housed the local Studebaker dealer. Mark and a friend climbed into his truck and we followed them down the

graveled original alignment to a bridge about five miles away where Mark talked excitedly about the nearby markers, the bridge and the highway. I had visited the bridge in 2009 but that was a couple of months before the markers

Mark at bridge west of Duncan, NE

were erected and I had made a short drive from the west side rather than following the old Lincoln Highway from Duncan. These really were new and interesting for me. I would be back here again in three days on a bus tour but that just wouldn't be as cool as the stop with just me, Paul, Mark and his buddy.

No one, particularly a group on a schedule, can stop at every interesting spot on the Highway. Everyone pretty much understands that but it doesn't make watching cars drive by – or not even get close to – things that are significant to you. I said this stop was partly sad. I was obviously referring to the fact that Mark had such a small audience for his enthusiasm and knowledge. I also mentioned it being encouraging and it really is encouraging to know there are folks like Mark who are proud of their area's connection to history and anxious to share it. There were a lot more people traveling the Lincoln Highway in its centennial year than our little troupe. I hope many more got a chance to meet Mark.

I stopped on the way into Grand Island to fill up at Kensinger's station. The Valiant's fuel tank and modern automatic shut-offs do not always get along so I usually just listen closely and detect a full

Dick Grudzinski fueling Valiant in Grand Island, NE

tank by the sound of gas in the filler tube. Since I wanted a picture of that rare full service, I asked manager Dick Grudzinski to put in ten gallons which I knew would fit. I stopped here in 2009 not too long after Rick Sebak's *A Drive Along the Lincoln Highway* was first broadcast. Dick and the station had appeared in the documentary and I asked him if it had helped business. There were more people taking pictures, he said, but there had been no great leap in actual business. He had not been impressed. I think that may have changed. The local visitors bureau has produced postcard style photos of Dick and the station where he is properly referred to as a "Local Lincoln Highway Icon" and he seems to be adjusting to that. I've a hunch that selling a little more gas to Lincoln Highway travelers has helped with the adjustment.

A unique bit of Lincoln Highway lies behind Kensinger's Station. In the 1910s, cement manufacturers teamed up with the LHA to create "seedling miles" to demonstrate the value of hard surface roads. One of those "seedlings" was right

Last unmolested seedling mile pavement

here and part of it still is. It is believed that this short portion of a

1915 "seedling mile" is the only one of its kind that has not been buried, widened, or otherwise molested.

From Kensinger's, I headed on to the motel where a great discovery awaited. My computer bag has a pocket on one side into which I often slip motel receipts and the like. I had a little trouble inserting the latest receipt and realized there was something in the pocket besides flat paper. There were my car keys. I must have dropped or laid them on the case where they slipped out of sight, possibly while I was jerking the case around to get at the spare set. Mystery solved.

From the motel, a bus took us on a tour of the town and delivered us to dinner at the recently restored and reopened Shady Bend restaurant. The tour included a stop at Kensinger's in the dusk when the neon was on. And that wasn't the only bonus. A rare 1948 Tucker automobile had joined the tour at Niland's in Colo, Iowa. The car would be driven in the parade in Kearney but would ride in a trailer until then. It did get out of the trailer for display at Niland's and again at Kensinger's. On both occasions, camera wielding tour members clustered around the car like

1948 Tucker at Kensinger's in Grand Island, NE

GIs around a 1940s pin-up model which is, of course, exactly what the Tucker is.

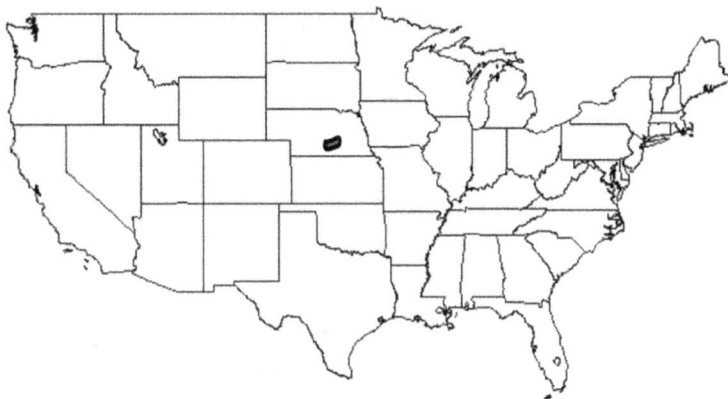

11 PARADE DAY

Victory, at least a little piece of it, was mine. The Valiant had made it to Grand Island, Nebraska, the last stop before Kearney. Half the wheel covers were in the back seat and dust from several states covered every surface but it had made it. And so had I. And so had both sets of keys.

I got up early and headed to a nearby coin operated car wash. Some had washed their cars the night before and needed just a little touch up in the morning. Some had lined up a hose at the motel and washed their cars there. Several were at the coin op place with me. I got the Valiant reasonably clean and got all the wheel covers back in place. It was not ready for the judges at a car show but it didn't look too bad. I returned to the hotel and, when cars started heading to the first staging area, I was ready.

Grand Island staging area

The cars were to be in model year sequence for the actual parade. There would be another staging area at the edge of Kearney for some fine tuning but the big shuffle needed to happen here. This was one of those times when I really appreciated being a peon and just being told where to be. I also deeply appreciate the non-peons who got all the ducks and Fords

Between Grand Island and Kearney

and Chevys and Packards and Plymouths in a row. Their job was made even tougher by the arrival of local cars which would be in the parade but were not to be mixed in with the tour cars. When we set out on the forty mile drive to Kearney, I was in my proper place between Don Reifsnyder's 1962 Corvette and Art Ackerman's 1963 Nova.

The final sequencing area was the parking lot of the Cabela's store on Kearney's east edge. This is also the parking lot for the Classic Car Collection museum which opened in a corner of the huge Cabela's building about a year and a half earlier. We had something like an hour until "show time" and were able to check out the museum once we were parked. The cars in the museum

Classic Car Collection, Kearney, NE

are primarily from the collection of Bernie and Janice Taulborg though a few other cars, including some loaners, are on display. It's an impressive collection.

The collection of cars lined up for the parade was also impressive. I believe that there were about fifty or sixty tour cars at this point and probably more "locals". When we left Grand Island, the Valiant had been the number ten car in

Final staging at Cabela's

line. It would leave Cabela's in the twelfth spot with the 1948 Tucker and a 1913 Stevens Duryea, which had been trailered in, added to the mix. At least two cars that should have been in front of me were not. One was the 1916 Oldsmobile that had been involved in the accident on the second day of the tour and the other was Andy Harvey's 1940 Zephyr that was out with a bad timing chain. It was Andy who had alerted us to our brake light problems back in Ohio.

I now discovered another problem. One that was potentially worse and one that could have kept the Valiant out of the parade. At some point, as I walked among the staged cars, I looked back at the Valiant and noticed a dark spot underneath it. I was aware of some minor oil leakage but it was not the sort that would make a six inch diameter spot in half an hour. It was a leaking fuel pump. Gasoline spreads quickly making a sizable spot from a small leak but even small fuel leaks are not to be ignored. Consultation with a couple of other drivers convinced me that there was little likelihood of a fire. The leak was low and well away from the exhaust. Parking the car would have been prudent but I couldn't bring myself to voluntarily drop out of the parade at this point. Dropping out involuntarily was a different thing and there was no doubt that a faulty fuel pump could very well make that happen. I had recently sensed just a little roughness in the car's idling and I now attributed that to the failing pump. There was no problem when in motion or in neutral with the revs cranked up just a bit.

The parade up Central Avenue would be the day's big event but first the two tour groups had to finish driving their halves of the

Lincoln Highway. Our departure from the lot was synchronized with the other group so that we would reach the center of town at the same time. It was a true "east meets west" occasion when we met and drove past cars that had traveled from San Francisco while we were driving from New York City. At our last drivers meeting, someone suggested that, rather than just waving to our west coast counterparts, we greet them with a Lincoln Highway 'L' formed with thumb and forefinger and that's just what we did.

East meets West in Kearney, NE

Following the drive-by, we moved to one more staging area where we would await our turn to join the real parade. As we turned left off of the Lincoln Highway, my right front wheel cover turned a little slower than the rest of the car and rolled off into someone's yard. Although the detaching of both right side wheel covers when I veered off road in Indiana is my only previous mention of the wheel covers going off on their own, it wasn't the only time it had happened. On the drive to New York, each of the right side covers had left me once. The front had made a run for it in Zanesville, Ohio, and the rear took off on its own just a block from the hotel in Secaucus. Until that scary day in Indiana when they both moved to the back seat, John and I made a habit of making sure the covers were firmly seated at almost every stop. I intended to bump them a bit before we left Cabela's but perhaps the fuel pump situation made me forget. I pulled over and got out of the car but before I had much of a chance to move, an onlooker ran up with the wheel cover in hand. Many thanks to the unknown bystander. The wheel cover was returned to the back seat and I raced off (relatively speaking) to regain my spot.

Driving the parade route was not the most relaxing thing I've ever done. I did punch the transmission into neutral a few times so I could keep engine RPMs up without running into the car in front of

Centennial Parade in Kearney, NE

me. Fear of the car simply dying was ever present and, despite my confidence that it would not happen, thoughts of the Valiant bursting into flames in downtown Kearney could not be kept completely at bay. But even the most horrifying possibilities couldn't keep me from enjoying the fantastic real world experience.

About 140 cars had participated in the centennial tours. Not all of them were present in Kearney but the majority certainly were. With the additions of local groups and individuals, the number of antique and classic cars in town today was estimated at between 450 and 500. There had been plans to arrange the cars so that each block contained a different decade. Sheer numbers made that entirely unrealistic. The announced parade attendance was 12, 500. The population of the city of Kearney is a little more than thirty thousand.

My personal reality was that my old car had made it across half the country and was part of the celebration for the old road. When I parked it, I could not be certain that it would move from the spot under its own power at the end of the day but I didn't really care.

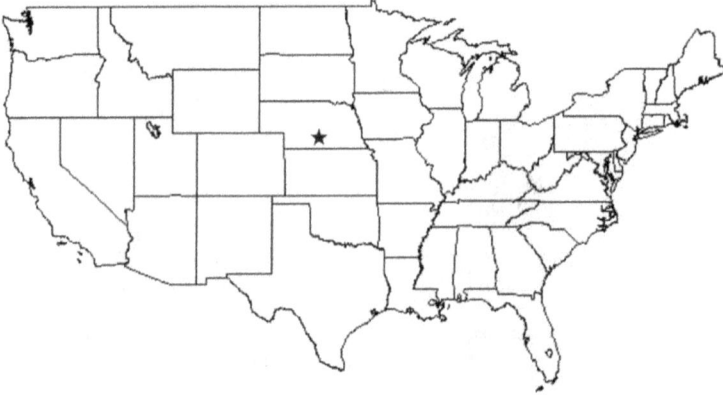

12 FIXES AND FESTIVITIES

The parade continued long after the tour cars were parked and I walked back to Central Avenue to watch some of it roll by. I walked around the crowded downtown, exchanged greetings with some of the west coast people, and just generally enjoyed the festive goings on. Eventually things began slowing down and I noticed a few cars leaving the display area. I was close behind. The Valiant started easily and carried me to the hotel without a hiccup. Then, in my room, I discovered a totally new problem.

The cooling fan in my computer had been making some noises on occasion. It made no noise now. It did not turn at all. Repeatedly cycling power resulted in only a couple of beeps and a "Fan Error" message. Though simultaneously having car problems and a dead computer might have easily led to being a little depressed, I was anything but. The satisfaction of making it to Kearney and the excitement of the parade left no room for depression. I used my phone to catch up on email and relaxed a bit in the room until time to head to the tour wrap up party.

As mentioned earlier, there were three components in the Lincoln Highway doings in Kearney. These were the car tours coming from the coasts, the centennial celebration, and the annual Lincoln Highway Association conference. Boundaries between the three were far from rigid and sometimes hardly discernible. Sunday's parade and associated festivities were part of the centennial celebration. It would continue on Monday, the actual anniversary of the incorporation of the original Lincoln Highway Association, with numerous activities at the Great Platte River Road Archway on Kearney's east side. While the two tours could be considered over when they met each other in downtown Kearney, each tour continued as a group through the parade that followed and the official disbanding would be marked by a Sunday night gathering. The celebration's second day would overlap the first day of the conference. Conference registration, setting up displays and the book room, and a board meeting all took place on Monday.

So it wasn't all that shocking when attendance at the wrap up shindig went well above the 250 or so tour participants in Kearney. Even though general conference activities would not start until Tuesday, almost everyone traveling to Kearney for the conference did so a couple of days early to get in on the parade and events at the Archway. It was, of course, a natural thing for those early arrivals to join the group of LHA members they saw eating and drinking and yakking like all good LHA members do. None of this fazed primary organizer Rosemary Rubin even a little. She arranged for a few more tables and chairs and a few more hors d'oeuvres and the cash bar took care of itself. A good time was had by all.

What was a little shocking, at least to me, was that the centennial books Brian Butko had "previewed" back in Pittsburgh had indeed arrived and were available. A little expediting has clearly taken place. Though I opted not to stand in line to pick it up that night, it was good to know that I would not have to wait to get home to see it.

Conference attendees were spread over three hotels. Some stayed at the Holiday Inn which was the official hotel where presentations and such took place. Others stayed at the neighboring Wingate and Hampton hotels. I was in the Wingate.

It was still light out when I headed across the parking lot to my hotel. Art Ackerman's 1963 Nova, which had been just behind me in the parade, was parked beside the Valiant and Art was nearby when I approached. Art and I had talked about my fuel pump situation and he now asked when I was going to start the job of replacing it. I suppose I had been avoiding thinking about it and replied something about doing it "tomorrow". Art commented that a couple hours of daylight remained and added that he would be willing to give me a hand if I wanted to tackle it now. I believe he also said something about seeing what surprises were waiting. Fortunately, I wasn't dumb enough to turn down his offer and his comment about surprises sure was insightful.

Milton Wheeler, who I would get better acquainted with as we both headed west after the conference, joined us. Milton was driving – and maintaining -- a 1947 Packard. Only a little of the help Art and Milton provided was hands on but their advice and suggestions were invaluable. Their matter of fact just-do-it attitude helped a bunch and it soon became obvious that Art's readiness to dive in had saved me from my own procrastination. I had naively envisioned simply unbolting the old pump and bolting on the new one. When the possibly fifty year old fuel line twisted into a useless tangle, Art or Milton or maybe both said, "Yeah. That happens a lot." When I headed to my room, the new pump was in place and I knew what I needed to buy.

Before going to sleep, I located some auto parts stores and a couple of computer repair shops. In the morning, I hit the phone as early as I thought reasonable. There was one parts store in walking distance and I called it first. Although allowing that a rubber line could be used if necessary, both Art and Milton had strongly suggested steel fuel line if possible. The nearby store only carried rubber. In hindsight, I might not have asked all the right questions because after a couple more phone calls and a little web searching, I learned that, while fuel lines and brake lines are technically different, most parts stores only carry brake line since tubing capable of handling the high pressure of braking is more than strong enough to handle the much lower pressure of fuel delivery. But, rather than retrying the nearby store, once I had found a place where I could get appropriate tubing, I moved on to my computer problem.

The first place I called told me to bring it in and they would run diagnostics on it for three days. They would then order any needed parts which would probably arrive in a couple of days. Then they would install them. I tried again to explain that I pretty much knew what was wrong and that I was a visitor in Kearney. My schedule did not really have room for their three day diagnostic period. The voice said "Sorry", though I did not sense much sympathy, "that's our policy."

Things went much better with the second call. Bring it on in, they told me. The sooner the better and they thought they could at least take a look at it today. Maybe even fix it today. I next called Mike Curtis, who had been next to me when the leak was discovered and who had offered his assistance, to arrange for some chauffeuring.

I had assumed that Mike and Sharon were attending the conference and had an essentially idle morning. I later learned that they were about to start their drive home to North Carolina but that didn't stop him from driving me to the computer shop and auto parts store.

That optimistic prediction on the computer turned out to be based on the erroneous belief that it was a desktop machine but my hope remained high. The two fellows in the store had the right attitude and an appreciation for my situation. They would look into getting a new replacement fan but feared that might take several days. They would also look for a suitable used fan in their "scrap box" in an effort to avoid a long delay. At the parts store, I bought the proper length of brake line with fittings, some rubber line just in case, and some much needed hand cleaner.

The Valiant's fuel pump mounts on the lower right of the engine. The carburetor is high on the left side. The path between them is a fairly intricate one around the front of the engine with numerous kinks and bends to bypass various obstacles. I discovered that the curved top of the radiator helped in starting bends without immediately crimping the tubing and commenced a long series of trials and errors. What I basically had to do was trace a three dimensional path with two dimensional bends and one dimensional visualization skills. Although the error to trial ratio was only slightly less than one to one, I did eventually get the two sides connected while keeping the line away from the fan and belt and other interesting features. The car started, ran smoothly, and didn't even squirt gas on the ground. I was once again mobile.

Seeing that it was not quite noon, I realized I had a chance to catch some of the day's festivities. I put the newly acquired hand cleaner to good use and got ready to head out to the Archway. I decided to drive around the parking lot a bit before putting the car on the street and that almost got me caught up in a Packard parade.

Some activities at the Archway had started at 9:00 AM but the Official Welcome & Centennial Ceremony was scheduled for 1:00. This ceremony would be immediately preceded by a parade of Packards that, as I now discovered, was forming in the Holiday Inn parking lot. As I satisfied myself that the Valiant was actually running OK, the line of a dozen or so classic Packards started toward the Archway and I had to alter my course to avoid getting caught up in it. I puttered around a bit longer then headed off after them.

The Great Platte River Road Archway is a huge building that sits atop Interstate 80. Entry is from the end at the northern edge of the expressway where tall escalators carry visitors to and from the museum area in the actual arch. A variety of exhibits, including life-size dioramas, costumed docents, and computer graphics present the history of transportation in America with an

Great Platte River Road Archway

emphasis on western expansion. Food service, a gift shop, and meeting/banquet areas fill the ground level space. The bulk of celebration related activities were arrayed in the general area around the Archway's entrance. In an effort to reduce congestion, parking at the Archway was restricted and visitors were asked to park at a remote lot to be shuttled to the party. That restriction did not, however, apply to cars that had participated in the centennial tour.

I was waved through the gate but the fellow doing the waving was not able to tell me where I should park. A young man near the Archway could not help me either. My guess is that knowledgeable volunteers had been in place when the bulk of the cars had arrived but had been relieved by the time I straggled in. I drove on past the Archway entrance. Seeing nothing at all promising on the east side of the building, I decided that the lot I had seen on the west side had to be it and headed back. As I drove very slowly through the people lining the street and occasionally crossing it, I realized that a couple of those people were calling out to me and I stopped the car to hear what they were saying. When I did that, a fellow walked up, removed the keys dangling from the trunk lock, and handed them to me. After discovering the lost set of keys two nights before, I had not returned the spare set to a safe place but had simply been walking around with both sets in my pocket and using whichever one came to hand. I had obviously last unlocked the trunk with one set then, in the excitement of having a running car, put the other set in the ignition and drove off. I found a parking spot in a lot on the west side of the Archway, put the spare keys in my camera case, and set off to see the festivities.

The official centennial ceremony was underway in a large tent across a bridge to the north. The tent was already filled so I could not get much of a view or hear much of what was said but at least I was there. And I heard enough to realize that someone was reading the US Senate "birthday resolution".

Official LHA Centennial Ceremony

The resolution had been introduced by both of Nebraska's senators and had passed unanimously on June 26. The resolution began by "Recognizing June 30, 2013, as the centennial of the Lincoln Highway...". A few paragraphs later it notes that "...on October 31, 1913, this great highway became the first national memorial to the 16th President of the United States, Abraham Lincoln...".

There are several significant dates in Lincoln Highway history. The night of October 31, 1913, is when the highway was dedicated with bonfire lit celebrations in cities all along its recently announced route. They got that one right. The Lincoln Highway Association, who laid out the route that was dedicated in October, was incorporated on July 1, 1913, and it is the centennial of that event that is being celebrated in Kearney. They missed it by **that** much but nobody really cared. There was a two day party going on and Lincoln Highway people welcomed the attention.

I was just getting fragments of whatever ceremonial activities were happening in the tent so I moved on to the Packards that were now parked in a big covered arc beyond the tent. Inside the arc was a 1917 Packard Twin Six once owned by Henry B. Joy. Joy was president of both the Packard Motor Car Company and the Lincoln Highway Association. The car,

Packards on display at Archway

on a trailer, had been in yesterday's parade through downtown Kearney and had led today's Packard parade to the Archway.

A couple of 1920s style campsites were set up at the east end of the line of Packards and I also looked them over. Then I headed back across the bridge thinking that I might go through the museum. Instead I spent some time just strolling around and chatting with new and old

1920s style auto camp

friends. I had enjoyed the museum when I was here in 2009 and knew I would enjoy it again but at the same time did not feel any strong need. So I walked and I talked.

One of the people I talked with was Brian Butko who had arrived that morning and who was signing and delivering copies of the centennial book that had gone from final edit to shipping in six days. Though the ink was barely dry, the books looked good and seeing the photos I had supplied, which did receive a little extra scrutiny from me, so nicely presented sure was satisfying.

The crowd in the tent thinned out considerably following the opening ceremonies and I eventually made my way back to it to catch a performance by vocalist Cece Otto. Cece, in period dress, has performed a number of concerts along the Lincoln Highway during its centennial year and has appeared at other Lincoln Highway functions including the 2011 and 2012 LHA conferences. I next went behind the tent to do something I've wanted to do for a long time.

Cece Otto at Centennial Celebration

Riding in a Model T Ford

My great-grandfather owned a Model T Ford when I was a kid. I remember the car quite clearly and sometimes think I rode in it and sometimes think I might have imagined that bit. But, regardless of whether my childhood rides were real or imagined, it was a certainty that I had not ridden in a Model T as an adult. Today I finally got my chance. Several T owners were offering rides along some dirt paths beyond the tent and I got in line. Before long I was climbing into a ninety-one year old automobile. It was an open four-door owned by a fellow named Ken. The rear seat held a man and wife and I sat in front beside Ken. I had intended to watch his feet as he operated those odd Model T pedals but instead found myself hooked on the view through the windshield as the agile little Ford bopped along the unpaved track.

I went back to walking and talking and trying to decide when to leave. The decision was made for me when the computer shop called to tell me my laptop was ready. They had not found a usable fan in the parts bin but they had managed to free up the old one with careful cleaning and discrete lubrication. It was not a permanent fix but it would likely get me through the trip and

Picking up the resurrected computer

a lengthy wait for parts was avoided.

While on a road trip, I maintain an online journal (some would say blog) with an entry for each day. Over the years, I have developed a routine that allows me to post an update each morning but there is not much slack. When something interferes and I get a little behind, it is nearly impossible to catch up. After picking up the computer, I immediately headed to the motel and started transferring pictures but I was almost back home in Cincinnati before the journal was current.

In the evening, I returned to the Great Platte River Road Archway for one more event. The Centennial Gala celebrated the Lincoln Highway Association's one-hundredth anniversary with dinner, local wines and beers, and a dance orchestra. I did not dance but I did celebrate the anniversary, the new fuel pump, the published photos, and the working computer.

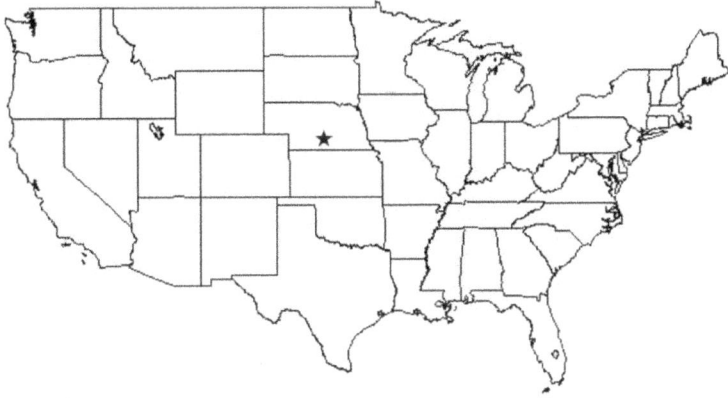

13 THE CONFERENCE

The last of the three events in Kearney was the annual Lincoln Highway Association Conference. Elements of the conference were spread over five days but the bulk of activities was concentrated on the middle three. As mentioned earlier, conference registration and a board meeting occurred on Monday. The general membership meeting would take place on Friday morning following a farewell breakfast. Bus tours, presentations, and banquets would fill Tuesday, Wednesday, and Thursday.

I took part in Tuesday's bus tour which ran east from Kearney. Having just driven to Kearney from that direction, I had seen many of the sites featured on the tour only days earlier but it was still fun to see them with the group and some expert

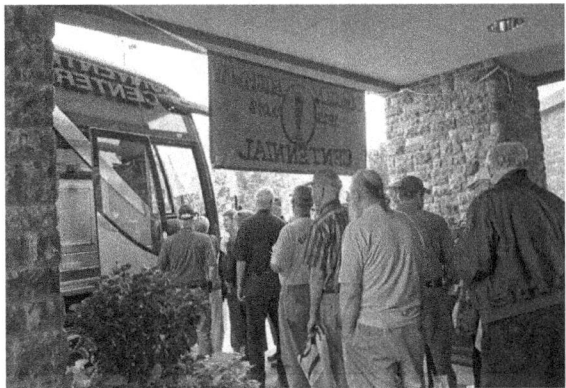

Boarding the tour bus

commentary. Plus the museum where we spent much of the afternoon was new-to-me and more than made up for the repeats.

First up was Kensinger's station and the "seedling mile" pavement behind it. This being my third visit in four days, the pavement had lost a little of its appeal and lost even more when hidden under a bus load of feet. So I quickly headed to the station

Dick Grudzinski at Kensinger's Station

which, along with manager Dick Grudzinski, had plenty of appeal left. I reached the station a little ahead of the crowd but it wasn't long before the little station was filled and Dick was surrounded by fans. The bus also stopped at the bridge west of Duncan that I had been personally guided to on Saturday then at the brew pub in Columbus where we had stopped for Saturday's afternoon break. This time our stop was for a full meal.

After lunch, we ventured away from the Lincoln Highway to the city of Lincoln, Nebraska, and the Museum of American Speed. The museum displays the collections of "Speedy" Bill Smith and, as the

Pedal cars at Museum of American Speed

museum's name and Bill's nickname suggest, it is about racing. At least it is mostly about racing. The displays of race cars and engines and all sorts of things that go with them is impressive. If that is all there was, the museum would be a very worthwhile stop but there is more; a lot more. There are huge collections of lunch boxes, model cars, soapbox derby racers, and on and on. Most impressive to me was the phenomenal collection of pedal cars. There are lots and lots of them including many that are extremely rare and unusual.

Wednesday was presentation day. The talks were informative, the handouts useful, and the slide shows enlightening but the highlight of the day for me was meeting Drake Hokanson. Drake wrote the first "modern" Lincoln Highway book back in 1988. Although, in the absence of other options, it was no doubt pressed into service as a sort of guidebook on occasion, that was never the intent. I believe that Drake considers himself a photographer first and a writer second so maybe the words in *Lincoln Highway: Main Street Across America* were there to support the pictures but it also works the other way around. I have read the book multiple times, including shortly before heading out on this centennial drive. There are more current and accurate books available, in particular those from Brian Butko, but Drake's twenty-five year old work always gets me in the mood to go out and see – and appreciate – the Lincoln Highway. And the photos are timeless.

Joyce Ausberger, Brian Butko, Kevin Patrick, Bob Ausberger, and Drake Hokanson

So I got to meet Drake Hokanson on Wednesday and I got my copy of *Lincoln Highway: Main Street Across America* autographed and I got to talk with him a couple more times before the conference ended and, yeah, he's a pretty cool dude.

The annual awards banquet took place Wednesday evening. As you might expect, there is a little "mutual admiration society" flavor to the proceedings but there is an even stronger sense of "mutual gratitude". The LHA operates entirely with volunteers and recognizing an accomplishment with a plaque or certificate is essentially a collective "thank you" for making this work for all of us.

LHA Awards Banquet

Wednesday was also Independence Day Eve and the date of the local Independence Day fireworks display. This was launched from a spot just across I-80 so, following the banquet, quite a few attendees joined other hotel guests, and probably a few locals, in the hotel parking lots for the show.

Independence Day Eve fireworks

There was another bus tour on Thursday, the Fourth of July, but I did not go. I was not alone in not registering for it. Two buses had been used on Tuesday's tour but there would be only one on Thursday. A couple smaller communities in the Kearney area had parades and other festivities scheduled and quite a few conference attendees planned to attend or even participate in one or the other of those. That had more or less been my intention when I had decided to skip the bus tour but I ended up finding nothing to do.

I don't mean I looked for something and didn't find it. I mean I looked for nothing and found it. After leaving home on June 19, I had been doing something for fifteen straight days. I was ready for a day off and this was it. I did do laundry and changed sparkplugs in the Valiant but I did both at a very leisurely pace. I even blew off a conference dinner at the Classic Car Collection museum. That was where the east tour had done our final sequencing on Sunday and I decided that I did not really need to see that collection again so soon and that driving out there was too much work. I completed my day off by walking to the pizza joint across the street. The conference would be completed with breakfast and a meeting in the morning.

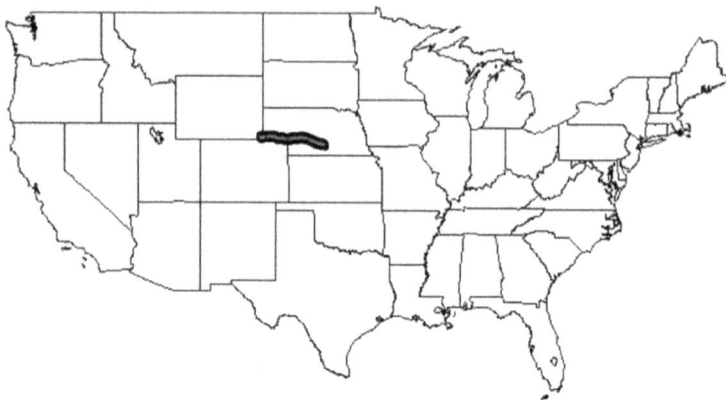

14 STARTING THE OTHER HALF

When I first thought of driving a fifty year old car on the one hundred year old Lincoln Highway, no end point other than San Francisco even entered my mind. It was only after talk of the two converging caravans started to circulate that I thought of Nebraska as anything other than just another state to pass through. And I still didn't plan to end my trip there. Even with Kearney as the end point of the official tours, I thought it likely that some number of folk from each tour would want to go on to the other coast. That's what I intended to do even if I was alone.

Apparently enough people asked about continuing or returning tours to have it included as an option when the time came to commit to the tour and sign up for motels. I, of course, signed on and checked off the list of motels that would see me to San Francisco. I joked about the possibility of the old car ending my trip at just about any point but it was only a joke. Going all the way on the Lincoln Highway was what I had in mind.

I guess it was that snafu with the plug wires on the eve of departure that got me to thinking just a little differently. Those jokes about the Valiant crapping out mid-trip had more than a drop of truth behind them, a truth that was reinforced by the incidents with the brake lights and fuel pump. My thoughts in Kearney were affected by this in two ways: 1) I realized how fortunate I had been to make it to the parade and celebration and knew that, although the west coast was still the goal, I would be satisfied if I got no further and 2) I was happy I would not be heading west alone.

It was not a large group and there was no chase vehicle as there had been on the main tours but there was a guide and a few other cars. Both Jim Peters, who had led the tour from New York City to Kearney, and Paul Gilger, who had done the same for the tour from San Francisco, had agreed to lead return tours back to their respective starting points. There may have been other cars that followed the Lincoln Highway from Kearney to one of the coasts but only three cars signed on to follow Paul all the way to San Francisco and no one signed on to caravan back to New York. Several other cars would hook up with us for various segments of the drive but only Milton and Carolee Wheeler, in a 1947 Packard, Rollie and Beth Roberts, in a 2007 Pontiac, and I, in the Valiant, would caravan all the way. Among the part-timers would be Jim Peters who, with no need to immediately head east, would work his way to the end of the Lincoln Highway in San Francisco. And caravan is, I believe, the right word. With a small group that never exceeded eight cars and normally numbered four or five, we really did travel as a single unit.

Because of the morning meeting, our first day's drive would be a relatively short one of just over a hundred miles to North Platte, Nebraska. We left Kearney around noon. The pace was leisurely with both planned and impromptu stops for photos and sightseeing. One

such stop was at the site of the former Covered Wagon Souvenir Shop next to what was once the 1733 Ranch. The ranch's name came from its location 1733 miles from both Boston and San Francisco. It became the traditional, though

Recently restored wagon & oxen near Kearney

not quite accurate, midpoint of the Lincoln Highway. The wagon and the critters pulling it had deteriorated rather badly over the years but were recently restored in anticipation of the highway's centennial. The coming centennial and the increase in travelers it was expected to bring prompted quite a few fix-ups and clean-ups along the route.

We stopped for lunch in Cozad and took in the 100th Meridian Museum while we were there. Cozad holds a little extra interest for me because it was founded by the same man who earlier founded a town near where I live named Cozaddale. Starting two towns is far from the only unusual thing that John J. Cozad did and his life story makes for some interesting reading. One of his sons gained fame as the painter Robert Henri and Cozad also contains a museum dedicated to him.

About ten miles beyond Cozad we moved onto the Gothenburg Steps. In the early part of the twentieth century, when the Lincoln Highway and other roads were being laid out, the natural thing to do was follow property and section lines. Of course this resulted in lots of right angle turns and, as the speed of automobiles increased, lots of accidents. These stair-like sections have long been eliminated from major routes by

Fort McPherson National Cemetery

turning them into gentle curves or bypassing them completely. Between Gothenburg and North Platte, the "steps" were left behind when the Lincoln Highway moved onto the Union Pacific right of way in 1917. Although today's pavement is much better than when the Lincoln Highway climbed these "steps", climbing them today provides a hint of what driving the old path was like. Fort McPherson National Cemetery lies about halfway up the "steps". It was established in 1873 on land once crossed by the Oregon Trail and the Pony Express.

We spent the night in North Platte though some of us drove out to Golden Spike Tower before ending the day. This eight story tower overlooks Bailey Yard. This is the world's largest train yard and the tall tower can make it feel like you are looking down on a super fancy model train layout but it is very real.

Golden Spike Tower, North Platte, NE

In the morning we stopped at Buffalo Bill's "Scout's Rest Ranch" just outside of North Platte. It was too early to visit the museum but we got some nice pictures in the morning light before moving on. A couple of miles further on we were driving atop the last section of the Lincoln Highway to be paved. That happened in 1935. In Ogallala we checked out a restored gas station from 1922 and stopped by the Boot Hill cemetery. The roughly 125 miles of Nebraska west of Ogallala is largely pleasant two-lane interrupted by nice looking small towns every ten or twenty miles.

Scout's Rest, North Platte, NE

We stopped for lunch in Sidney then, at approximately 3:30 in the afternoon, I left Nebraska for the first time in seven days.

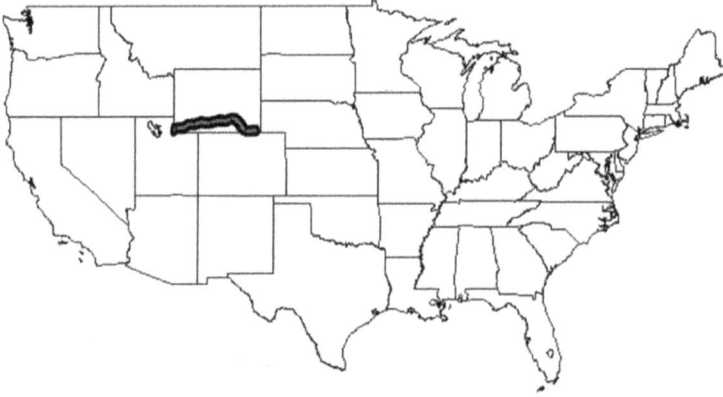

15 WYOMING

I don't know where the American West begins although some people seem to have it nailed down pretty good. Fort Worth, Texas, calls itself the city "Where the West Begins", the 100th meridian, which passes through the town of Cozad and more or less defines the east edge of the Texas panhandle, is popular and racer/writer Denise McCluggage once tied it to a specific bush near Santa Fe,

Cheyenne sign painter surveys his work on a sign with men in hats and boots riding horses

New Mexico, though her claim was pretty light hearted. To writer Drake Hokanson it must be Salt Lake City since Chicago and Salt Lake City are named as the separators when he describes the Lincoln Highway as a "three act play". The city where I live, Cincinnati, Ohio, was once called the "Queen City of the West" although I don't know of anyone actively promoting that today.

I'm not even sure what defines the American West but I sense that it involves hats, boots, and horses. If, as some say, the change started back in Cozad, it was quite subtle. By Cheyenne, it is subtle no more. So, I'm going to pick the Nebraska-Wyoming state line as the beginning of the American West on the Lincoln Highway. Your opinion might be different and, at some future date, so might mine.

Cheyenne is home to the historic Plains Hotel where I fully intend to stay someday but not this time. Just as they had been for the tours to Kearney, Holiday Inn discounts and group bookings had been available for the post-conference trips and I took advantage of that. I did, however, eat dinner at the 102 year old hotel. I guess my chicken and pasta washed down with a local craft beer wasn't a very cowboy-like meal but it sure was good. And I did eat it at the bar.

Plains Hotel, Cheyenne, WY

We left Cheyenne on a two-lane road but were on the interstate after about a dozen miles. Not only is part of the original Lincoln

Tree Rock between the lanes of I-80

Highway buried under I-80, one of Wyoming's more famous landmarks, Tree Rock, actually stands in the middle of the expressway. It is said that, when the railroad came through here in 1867, a small jog was made to save the little pine tree that looks as if it is growing from solid rock. The railroad eventually moved south and now it is Interstate 80 that jogs just a bit to preserve the tree between its east and west bound lanes.

Another major landmark, Ames Monument, stands at the end of a gravel road which I chose not to tackle in the Valiant but which some of the group did do. I have visited the monument in the past and have

Ames Monument (August 20, 2009)

included a photograph from 2009. The massive pyramid was built in 1882 to honor Oakes and Oliver Ames for their contributions to construction of the first transcontinental railroad and marked what was then the highest point on the route.

A couple of monuments with direct Lincoln Highway connections have been moved from their original locations to an I-80 rest area

and we visited both the monuments and the spots where they originally stood. One, a giant bust of Abraham Lincoln can be seen in its current location from its original location atop Sherman Summit. The other once marked the spot

Bust of Lincoln as viewed from Sherman Summit

where Lincoln Highway Association president, Henry B. Joy wanted to be buried but his family decided differently. It is quite a bit further west.

A picture taken in 2009 shows both monuments in their current setting at the Sherman Summit Rest Area. The Joy monument is

bordered by the same concrete posts used to mark the entire Lincoln Highway in 1928. A half dozen miles of expressway took us from the rest area to Laramie where we, and the Lincoln Highway, turned north. We would rejoin I-80 in about a hundred miles near the town of Walcott.

Sherman Summit Rest Area (August 20, 2009)

What we actually followed between Laramie and Walcott was US 30 which truly traces the Lincoln Highway in some spots but only approximates it in others. The Lincoln Highway was realigned more than once in this area and some of it simply no longer exists. Some of what does exist would require a high-clearance 4-wheel drive vehicle to negotiate plus some is now on private land.

The road passes a genuine one-stop, complete with gas, food, and lodging, at Rock River and the 104 year old Virginian Hotel, where we had lunch, in Medicine Bow. In between is what *Ripley's Believe It or Not!* called the "Oldest Cabin in the World", a house built of dinosaur bones.

Rock River one stop

Dinosaur bone house

Virginian Hotel

The weather was near perfect and the classic roadside attractions served to accent a very pleasant drive. The paved two-lane is a far cry from what carried drivers on the early Lincoln Highway so it took a little imagination to picture what those days were like but it took almost no effort at all to believe we were lost in the 1950s or '60s.

Following Paul Gilger's Mustang into the Wyoming sky near Medicine Bow

We reconnected with I-80 then exited long enough to drive through Rawlins. We exited again about thirty miles west of Rawlins to visit the original site of the Henry B. Joy monument that we saw back at Sherman Summit. Getting to what had been Joy's favorite spot on the highway involved a short drive on gravel but the view was more than worth it.

The Wheelers' Packard at original location of Henry B. Joy monument

Green River Palisades

The rest of our time in Wyoming was also a mixture of two-lane and expressway. We exited the interstate to drive through Rock Springs and Green River. We stopped to photograph the Green River Palisades and an abandoned gas station near James Town. A

QT's Packard and the Elderton's Model A Ford

photo taken at the station was the last I got of QT Freytag's 1949 Packard. A short time later the car became the group's only casualty when it suffered a broken rear axle. QT and his son, Caleb, had been part of the San Francisco to Kearney Centennial Tour and had been part timers in our west bound caravan.

When the breakdown was discovered, Paul and the Wheelers turned back to lend a hand while the rest of the group moved on to

Little America, an old and well known truck stop and motel, to wait – and eat ice cream. When the seriousness of the problem was realized, arrangements were made to truck the Packard back to Green River to await repairs. QT and Caleb stayed with the car.

We opted not to drive the gravel Lincoln Highway alignment just west of Little America but did go to the point where it splits off from US 30. Between this point and Philadelphia, Pennsylvania, US 30 essentially took over the route of the Lincoln Highway but the two parted ways here with US 30 heading off to ultimately reach Astoria, Oregon, and the Lincoln

Last LH marker in Wyoming at original location

Highway heading to Lyman, Wyoming. We did neither but returned to I-80 for a few miles to the Lyman exit. Before reaching Lyman, we stopped at the only 1928 concrete Lincoln Highway marker in Wyoming that remains at its original location. Then it was onto Fort Bridger where we looked over the Black and Orange tourist cabins which were restored a few years ago.

Black and Orange Cabins at Fort Bridger

Our last stop in Wyoming was at the roundhouse in Evanston. Evanston was once a major Union Pacific Railroad repair center with a huge roundhouse that the city now owns and is in the process of converting to their city hall. We got a guided tour of the facility and even got a ride on the big turntable that used to swing locomotives around to line them up with repair stations.

Roundhouse, Evanston, WY

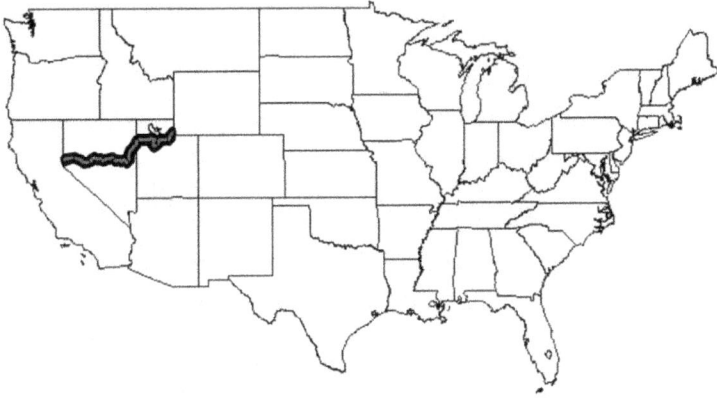

16 UTAH & NEVADA

The Lincoln Highway enters Utah in that notch made by Wyoming in the northeast corner. At the point of entry, the western border is barely a hundred and fifty miles away. Or it would be if you could drive due west which, of course you can't because the Great Salt Lake lies dead, literally, ahead. But things got squirrely even before the road reached the lake. The Proclamation Route, the first route announced by the Lincoln Highway Association in 1913, did not go through Ogden. Utah's governor raised a ruckus and an Ogden Loop was added. It was gone when the first official guide was published in 1915.

Beyond the lake, which the route passed by on its southern tip, the Great Salt Lake Desert and other problems with the terrain were added to the political issues and the routing shenanigans grew even more "interesting". The Lincoln Highway went through three basic alignments and innumerable small adjustments in getting from Salt Lake City to Ely, Nevada. If you want to understand the Lincoln Highway in Utah, you're going to need a bigger book.

Deciding what path we were going to follow was not particularly tough. No one really even considered the short lived Ogden Loop so we took a direct route from the border to our motel in Tooele on the west side of Salt Lake City. Big portions of both the original and second alignments west of the lake became inaccessible in 1942 when they were made part of the Dugway Proving Ground. Other portions are accessible but unpaved and pretty rugged. Some members of the eastbound centennial tour had taken that original path because it is, after all, the alignment of a hundred years ago, but no one in our little group felt the urge to do it. I certainly didn't. I drove it once in an all wheel drive SUV and knew that an old Valiant simply did not belong out there. That left the third and final alignment through Wendover as our only sensible choice but we would not follow it rigidly. A couple pieces of history near the eastern end of the old alignments can be easily reached on paved roads so, while we would basically follow the final Lincoln Highway alignment across the Great Salt Desert, we would cherry pick some of the older stuff, too.

The first of these was Fisher Pass where a new marker stands. This was part of the second alignment known as the Goodyear Cutoff. The name was changed from Johnson Pass to honor Lincoln Highway Association founder Carl Fisher and a monument to Fisher was to have been built here along with major improvements to the road through

Fisher Pass Monument

the pass. Neither the improvements nor the monument were completed as the Lincoln Highway Association and the state of Utah had agreed. Over the last one hundred years, much of the road has been improved and paved but the monument only

Devil's Gate Narrows in Fisher Pass
(photo by Carolee Wheeler)

became a reality in 2009 as the result of efforts by LHA member Roland Southwell who passed away in March of 2013.

We stayed with the second alignment until it intersected the first then drove a short distance south to Orr's Ranch. This was a well known stop where early Lincoln Highway travelers could get a meal or gasoline or even spend the night.

The caravan at Orr's Ranch

From the ranch we drove north on the original alignment which is the direction of the earliest eastbound Lincoln Highway traffic. These days, Interstate 80 is the active path over the salt flats with the former US 40, unmaintained and mostly unused, crumbling beside it. We crossed, slowly and carefully, on the old road then paid a visit to Bonneville Salt Flats International Speedway.

Crossing salt flats on Old US 40

The actual
Speedway, the area
used for attacking
various speed
records, lies well
beyond where the
pavement ends.
When it is dry,
nothing prevents
visitors from driving
onto the salt though
it is clearly "at your
own risk". I once

Pirates of Bonneville

drove about a half mile off the pavement just so I could say I did.
When it is wet, nothing but common sense prevents visitors from
driving onto the salt and not everyone will let that get in the way of a
good time.

From Wendover, actually West Wendover, in Nevada, our route
was almost directly south on what is now US 93. This was one of the
last alignments approved by the Lincoln Highway Association. When
the Association
adopted the route to
Wendover, this drop
to the south became
necessary to connect
with the rest of the
Lincoln Highway to
the west. The road
appears fairly level
but is, in fact, an
almost steady climb
towards the base of

Pointed south on US 93 in Nevada

Ward Mountain.
The temperature
was in the 90s. The hopped up Model A of part time caravan
members Chuck and Nora Elderton did boil over at one point and I
kept a nervous eye on the temperature gauge. The old Valiant
benefited from the stop to tend to the Model A and even more so
from a simple rest stop a bit further on.

The end of the day found us in Ely, Nevada, with rooms at the historic Hotel Nevada. At 6 stories, the hotel was the tallest building in the state of Nevada when it opened in 1929. This was the only time on the west bound portion of the trip that I stayed in anything other than a Holiday Inn or affiliate. As explained earlier, this was for

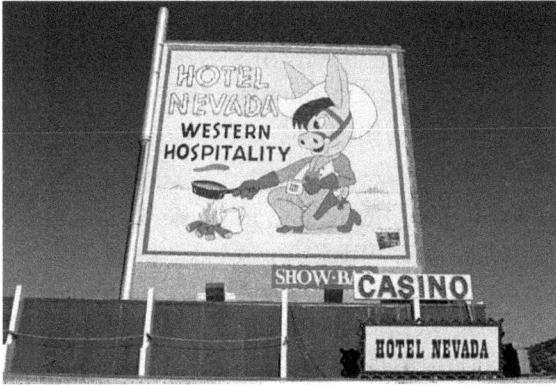

Hotel Nevada, Ely, NV

the simplified booking resulting from arrangements made between the Lincoln Highway Association and the hotel chain and for the convenience of staying with the group. Ely, Nevada, was the only overnight stop where Holiday Inn had no presence. That was just fine with me because I like staying in historic hotels but it does emphasize the point that Ely is a little more isolated than most of our overnight stops. It is, in fact, on The Loneliest Road in America.

The Loneliest Road in America is what *Life Magazine* called Nevada's portion of US 50 back in 1986. The road isn't all that lonely these days and the name might have faded away if it wasn't such a darned catchy slogan for attracting tourists. US 50 reaches Ely from the east in the company of US 6. US 6 turns southwesterly at the edge of town while US 50 runs right through downtown and continues west. US 93 basically passes through town and continues south but all three US routes do run

Soon after leaving Ely, the Valiant hit the jackpot

together for a short distance. The Lincoln Highway makes not a turn as it passes through Ely but the number of the route it is travelling with changes from 93 to 50.

Parts of the drive to Fallon, Nevada, our next overnight stop, may or may not be lonely but there is no question it is scenic. At 259 miles, the run to Fallon is the second longest one day drive for the Kearney to San Francisco caravan. The towns of Eureka, Austin, and Middlegate divide the distance into four segments of fifty to seventy miles. In between, there is little along the road other than scenery but the road itself seldom seems empty.

Eureka and Austin are legitimate towns with multiple businesses such as restaurants, bars, and motels. Eureka even has a nicely restored opera house. The International Hotel in Austin no longer rents rooms but it still has a bar on one side and a restaurant on the other which is where we ate lunch. Middlegate, on the other hand, is essentially a bar, restaurant, small motel, and campground all rolled into one. It is a great place for a beer and a 'burger

The caravan in Eureka, NV

but Middlegate's best known feature is not exactly in Middlegate. I'll get to that later.

I have driven the Lincoln Highway through here twice in the past. Both times I stayed on US 50 which is identified as the Lincoln's original

International Hotel in Austin, NV

alignment. State route 722, which turns south from US 50 just west of Austin, is identified as the second generation alignment. I have no idea why I did not follow this road on one of my previous passes but that is what we did today and I was blown away. The pavement is in good condition although signs declaring "MINIMAL MAINTENANCE" reinforce the idea that this is not the primary route in these parts. It climbs up and down and twists and turns for about sixty miles before reconnecting with US 50. This is clearly not the express route. This is the scenic route.

About twenty miles after swinging onto 722, we pulled to the side of the road. One reason was to look over the scenery which included a salt flat straight ahead. The salt flats here are nowhere near as big as what we crossed in Utah but they are still rather large. From a

Approaching a Nevada salt flat
(photo by Carolee Wheeler)

distance they look like frozen lakes. The salt radiates absorbed heat that can actually be felt when passing close by. But studying the countryside was not the primary reason for stopping. The tops of the other two convertibles in the group, Paul's Mustang and the Roberts' G6, had been going up each afternoon. Mine stayed down. They had air conditioning; I did not. Once or twice, Paul had said something about the top blocking the sun but I more or less ignored him and kept the top folded. So, as we got ready to move on, two tops went up and Paul repeated his comment about the sun. As I prepared to depart with my top still down, Paul made a motion with his head indicating that I ought to reconsider. Then he waited. The message, I think, was "I can't make you put the top up but I can remain here until you do." I put the top up and did not regret it for a minute. The air still flowed through the open windows and being shielded from the Nevada sun was a good thing. Even stubborn old men can be retrained on occasion.

The abandoned Carroll Station is roughly three miles from Carroll Summit. We paused there for a pleasant break under the shade of some trees. Carroll Station operated from around 1925, when the Lincoln Highway (soon US 50) was routed through here, until around 1962 when US 50 moved close to the original Lincoln Highway alignment where it remains today. We stopped again, just beyond the 7425 foot summit, to get a look at the road looping and wiggling its way down the

Taking a break at Carroll Station

Second alignment of Lincoln Highway descending west side of Carroll Summit

west slope. After getting several views and pictures from different spots, we started on down those loops and wiggles.

Near the bottom, just a few miles before reaching US 50, we stopped at Eastgate. Over the years, a pony express station, a stage coach stop, and a Lincoln Highway era roadhouse have operated here. Remnants of all three can be seen.

Pony Express station ruins at Eastgate

Barely a mile after returning to US 50, we pulled over to check out one of those odd specimens of roadside flora, a shoe tree. There are several shoe trees in the United States and even a few different varieties. The most common variety is one into which people toss pairs of shoes tied together so they can dangle from the branches. A large shoe tree can bloom with hundreds of shoes. Individual shoe trees usually have a colorful story (or

The highest shoes in the trees on July 10, 2013

two or more) about how they got started but I've found nothing on why or where the very first of the breed appeared. Until the night of December 30, 2010, what some called the world's tallest shoe tree stood beside US 50 just a couple of miles east of Middlegate Station. Because of its proximity, the tree was often referred to as the Middlegate Shoe Tree which I hope explains my earlier comment about Middlegate's best known feature not being in Middlegate. Sometime during that December night, unknown persons brought the tree down, presumably with a chain saw. Why anyone would want to do that is a mystery but what makes people want to throw shoes into a tree is not well understood, either. Although they are no match in height for the big cottonwood, which was described as 70 or 80 feet tall, two neighboring trees were quickly pressed into service as replacements.

A pause for refreshments at Middlegate

As the existence of Middlegate implies, there is a Westgate though nothing marks the spot. The names come from Captain James Simpson who was the first to survey a route through this area to establish a shorter way west than the existing trail along the Humboldt River. He referred to mountain passes as "gates" and identified an Eastgate, a Westgate, and a Middlegate.

Our last stop of the day was at Sand Mountain Recreation Area. The huge sand dunes, with people darting around them on motorcycles and ATVs, were pretty cool but I think it is even cooler that Jeff Prince showed up while we were there and I got a picture of his "Family Truckster". My first encounter with the Truckster was back at the Sherman Summit rest area. The photo gives me an opening to write about it here.

Jeff, Demetria, and the Family Truckster

Not only is 2013 the centennial of the Lincoln Highway, it is the 30th anniversary of the movie *National Lampoon's Vacation* starring Chevy Chase. The movie featured an over-the-top station wagon known as the Wagon Queen Family Truckster. Jeff did a little makeover on a station wagon he already owned so that it resembled the Truckster and set out on a road trip with girlfriend Demetria Perkins. But it was not just any old road trip. Jeff is a fan of old roads and a member of the Lincoln Highway Association. His dream road trip was one that went coast to coast on the Lincoln Highway.

For a twenty-something to have an attraction to and knowledge of the Lincoln Highway is rather unusual. It is not unusual for a twenty-something to otherwise have different interests and a different budget than the "slightly older" travelers in the caravan. Jeff and Demetria had started in New York on the same day as the centennial tour and sort of shadowed it. They spent most nights in the same cities as the tour but in different motels. Where possible, they slept and ate in locally owned mom-and-pop establishments. Their daily start and end points might be the same as the group's, but the paths often differed as they explored places like Pittsburgh or Chicago.

I had seen the Family Truckster in Kearney but did not know its story or give it much thought. Although meeting Jeff and Demetria at the rest area had been a first for Paul as well, he was familiar with what they were doing and invited them to travel with us. They had become part time caravaners.

We ended the day in Fallon where I had to stop by the Overland Hotel even though we were not, of course, staying there. The hotel was built in 1910 and was ready and waiting when the Lincoln Highway was routed by its front door three years later. I have stayed at the Overland and would do so again but I can't really recommend it for the typical traveler.

Overland Hotel, Fallon, NV

The bathroom is shared and everything is rather primitive.

In the morning, we headed onto Reno and the remarkable National Automobile Museum. The museum houses what is essentially the remains of casino owner Bill Harrah's car collection and that is often the way people refer to it. I believe it is on every top ten car museum list ever compiled since it opened in 1989. I had missed a couple of opportunities to see it in the past and was looking forward to seeing it today. Even with high expectations, I was very much impressed. One of the museum's most famous cars is the Thomas Flyer that won the 1908 New York to Paris Automobile Race. The car has been restored to exactly the same condition

Thomas Flyer at National Automobile Museum

as when it won what is frequently referred to as "The Great Race".

We made one more stop before slipping over the California line. One of the best known bridges on the Lincoln Highway is the one in Tama, Iowa, with "LINCOLN HIGHWAY" cast into each railing. It is sometimes said that those are the only ones like that or that

Beth & Rollie Roberts, Me, Carolee & Milton Wheeler, Jim Peters, Paul Gilger
(photo by Tucker the Trucker)

they are the oldest. Neither is true. The Tama bridge was built in 1915 and modeled after a bridge built near Reno, Nevada, the year before. That earlier bridge was over a small culvert and just long enough to accommodate one word of the name on each side. The one in Iowa, over Mud Creek, was long enough for each railing to spell out the full name. Railings from the abandoned culvert were rescued in the 1970s and moved to an I-80 pull-out about a mile west of their original location. The pull-out is accessible only from eastbound I-80.

We made our way to the pull-out and commenced our usual routine of milling around and taking pictures. The pull-out provides quite a bit of parking for trucks and one was parked there today. Its driver was killing time before the scheduled arrival at his destination and walked over to see what we were looking at. He did not know much about the Lincoln Highway but seemed genuinely interested and asked a few sincere questions. Noting that we were all taking pictures he offered to take a picture of the whole group. We had actually been talking about that and took him up on his offer immediately. We thanked him and asked his name. "Tucker", he said. The Truckee River flows a few hundred yards behind the pull-out. The town of Truckee is just a couple dozen miles to the west. I, like other solo drivers (I assume/hope), do sometimes have silly thoughts as I motor along but most are just between me and the steering wheel. Maybe it was entering this trip's twelfth and final Lincoln

Highway state that made me a little extra goofy. Whatever the reason, by the end of the day I had shared the day's silly thoughts on the internet and, since they have already been broadcast into the ether, I might as well share them here:

> *Met a trucker named Tucker near Truckee.*
> *Knew at once that our meeting was lucky.*
> *'Cause we wanted a shot*
> *Of the whole bloody lot*
> *And the one that he took was just ducky.*

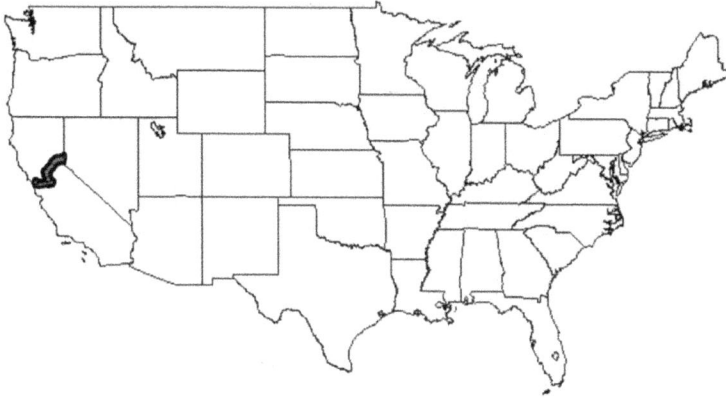

17 CALIFORNIA

We actually entered California twice. Once near Verdi, Nevada, on a road that, just a bit further on, would become much rougher than we were prepared to deal with, then for real on Interstate 80. This was not due to a bad decision and a retreat but a planned maneuver to let us see the state line on the original Lincoln Highway routing without getting in over our heads. On the old alignment, we turned around just beyond a cast iron obelisk with one side marked "NEVADA", the opposite side marked "CALIFORNIA", and a third proclaiming "LONGITUDE 120 WEST OF GREENWICH". The words are correct; the number not quite.

1872 Nevada-California border marker

When California became a state in 1850, this section of its eastern border was defined as 120 degrees west longitude. Several surveys were conducted to find this theoretical line with no two agreeing. The one that Alexey Von Schmidt did in 1872 might not have been any more accurate than the others but he did one thing differently. In addition to sticks and stones, Von Schmidt used iron posts such as this one to mark his version in several spots. This is the only one known to survive. Subsequent surveys revealed that Von Schmidt's survey erred by several hundred feet and made California a little skinnier than intended. Neither state cared enough to move the markers and the 1872 line became the real line. LONGITUDE 120.00186 WEST OF GREENWICH is close enough.

Back on I-80, we exited at Floriston, just a few miles over the line, to explore some abandoned 1926 Lincoln Highway. This alignment once also carried US 40 and was once paved. Although it has mostly reverted to dirt, the surface is quite drivable and looks as though it might even be graded now and then. I took the opportunity to photograph the Valiant on the primitive roadway.

1926 alignment near Floriston, CA

We ate lunch at Jax Diner in Truckee. It is a 1948 Kuhlman diner that opened at its current location in 1995 after a relocation from Philadelphia, Pennsylvania. Good food and a spot on the Food Network's "Diners, Drive-ins, and Dives" keeps the place busy. It was busy enough while we were there that we began to worry about ticking parking meters but we all escaped without a ticket and headed off to Donner Pass.

Jax Diner, Truckee, CA

This was my second visit to the pass and this time I think I really started to understand the appreciation others express for this place. It seems there is just too much history, in too many layers, to process in

Donner Lake and Donner Pass Bridge

a single visit; two is not enough, either. As everyone knows, the notch in the Sierra Nevada gets its name from the group of emigrants who were stranded here in the winter of 1846 though neither they nor the wagon trains that preceded them were the first to make use of the pass. Numerous petroglyphs tell of a human presence here as many as 4000 years ago.

It's hard to believe but only a couple of decades separate the Donner-Reed party being halted here by snow and the first steam train rolling through. Creation of the required railway tunnels is, all by itself, a big chapter in the transportation story along with the

Railroad underpass (subway) near center of picture

building of gigantic supporting walls. Long snow sheds were constructed to keep the tracks clear. When the automobile and the Lincoln Highway came along, those sheds added to the already high risk involved in crossing railroad tracks. The first railroad underpass in the country was built here in 1914 to alleviate the danger. In 1926, the first inclined, curved, and banked bridge in the world made the road even safer and shorter. In between those years, the Lincoln Highway followed several alignments over the mountain and various remnants can still be seen. Plus there is that gorgeous lake. Yeah, I can see why so many put this spot at or near the top of their Lincoln Highway favorites list. I've now done that, too, though I am a few visits shy of absorbing all that is there.

On my first visit to Donner Pass, I did not cross the summit. The Lincoln Highway splits into a Northern and Southern (a.k.a. Pioneer) Route several miles west of Fallon. That first visit was with another Paul Gilger

The Roberts heading over Donner Summit

led group immediately following the 2011 Lincoln Highway

Conference at Lake Tahoe. I had reached the conference on the Southern Route and I returned to Lake Tahoe from the pass to continue west on the same route. Today we were following the Northern Route on through Donner Pass and I would get to see some very old new-to-me Lincoln Highway.

It was quite the scenic drive with tree lined curves and slopes that would not let me forget my manual drum brakes. Near the town of Newcastle, the actual pavement got interesting. First up was a location where four paving projects came together. Not only did paving from two directions join here, each lane was completed at different times. The evidence is in dates in the pavement showing when each of the four sections was completed. It was once common practice to stamp the date into newly poured concrete paving at the end of a project. The lanes coming from the northwest were completed on March 7 and March 31 of 1932. The others on May 7 and some day in April of 1934. Less than a mile later, Paul made a couple of turns and led us over some original concrete pavement from 1914.

One of four date stamps at paving joint

1914 concrete pavement near Newcastle, CA

Having all those bits of old road to look over made for a long day and it was dark by the time we reached our hotel in Sacramento. At the front desk, Paul explained that we were with the Lincoln Highway Association and gave his name.

"Oh, I've got something for you", the clerk announced and stepped into the little office off to the side. She emerged with what looked like a poorly made aboriginal fishing net as Paul's bewilderment grew. The clerk read from a note, "Someone named Freytag left this."

I was the only one who could have had any notion of what the thing was and it took me a few seconds to recognize it. When I did, I burst out laughing. The item in question was one of the cheap seat pads that John and I had bought in Pennsylvania on the second day of the tour. Back in Ogallala, Nebraska, QT and I were talking as we stood by the cars. He noticed the pad and asked if it helped.

"A little", I answered and suggested he give it a try since it was going unused. I had never worried much about ever getting it back and not at all after QT's trip was cut short by the broken axle. I don't know whether QT stayed at the hotel or just stopped by. Regardless, he had passed through Sacramento and, knowing we would soon be there, dropped off the pad. Not sure of my last name, he left it for a much surprised Paul.

From Sacramento, just 145 miles of Lincoln Highway remained. The weather, as it had been on so many days of the trip, was great as we drove past California's capitol and left the city in a slightly southeasterly direction. Two distinct Lincoln Highway alignments lead from Sacramento to San Francisco. The final one, the one marked by concrete posts in 1928, is a fairly straight line between the cities that became possible only after the Carquinez Strait was bridged in 1927. The original route, the one we were following, ran south, with a slightly eastern slant, until turning west a dozen miles or so south of Stockton. We made brief photo stops in Galt, Woodbridge, and Stockton.

Galt historical marker

Woodbridge

Stockton Hotel

We ate lunch at a fun little place in Tracey. It was our last meal as a group and we stretched it out just a little. West of Tracey, the drive over Altamont Pass is quite pretty although I imagine it was even prettier before all those windmills appeared.

Altamont Pass

Our last stop as a caravan was at the Duarte Garage in Livermore where members of the historical society had the garage open and were on hand to show us around. Next stop, San Francisco.

I would be making one extremely brief stop before reaching the terminus marker in Lincoln Park. My oldest son, Crispian,

The Highway Garage of Livermore

lives in San Francisco and was working just a few blocks from the 1913 path of the Lincoln Highway up Market Street. Through the magic of cell phones, he would be waiting on a convenient corner and would join me for the last few miles. I took up the rear position when we left Livermore so that I could make any adjustments or retries necessary without involving anyone else.

Because of my own goof, I became separated from the group as we approached the Bay Bridge then ended up reaching downtown ahead of the caravan. I called Paul to apologize and to let him know where I was and that I would meet them at the marker. I picked up Cris without a problem and cruised on to Lincoln Park. The Golden Gate Bridge was on our right as we entered the park and I'm guessing that I was sporting a pretty big grin. I drove on past the terminus marker so I could turn around and pull up in front of it. Cris climbed out and snapped a picture. It had been six or seven years since I'd first thought of pulling up to this marker in a fifty year old car and actually doing it felt marvelous.

Mission accomplished
(photo by Crispian Gibson)

It was a really nice surprise to see the Family Truckster already in the park. We had not seen it recently as Jeff and Demetria followed their own schedule. They had reached the park about ten minutes before I did. In a few more minutes, the rest of the caravan began arriving. Crispian was drafted as our photographer and a group of very happy people crowded around the concrete post. The Wheelers had travelled across the country so they could drive back. They and Paul were essentially home. The rest of us still had to get back to Massachusetts, Iowa, South Carolina, and Ohio. So what?

Demetria, Jeff, Rollie, Milton, Carolee, Paul, Jim
Me, Beth
(photo by Crispian Gibson)

18 THE AFTERPATH

I did it. I drove my Mopar to the Golden Gate or at least to a park overlooking the Golden Gate. There was, however, one little celebratory activity remaining. Early travelers often celebrated a crossing of the continent by a dipping of their front wheels in the Pacific and a meal at the Cliff House. It is no longer possible to get a car to the water but the Cliff House is still very much there.

There were three of us. Jim Peters, who had led the New York to Kearney and had been with our little caravan at the end, joined Crispian and me and we all celebrated with great food and marvelous views. When I had at last become convinced that I would reach San Francisco, I called a favorite motel only to learn it was all but filled. The lone opening was a two room suite at a rate well above

Sunset from the Cliff House

what I was willing to pay. Then I spoke with Jim, who had been calling other motels in the area without success. Splitting the suite would solve both of our problems so I quickly called back to the motel and made the reservation.

I had been telling my son he should plan on getting home on his own. I did not know how well the Valiant would be running and I did not relish driving it through the city at night. After dinner, I relented. The car was performing quite well and I, helped no doubt by the fine meal, was in a good mood. We all climbed into the Valiant and headed toward downtown.

The drive to Crispian's apartment was without incident. We said our goodbyes and headed back up Geary toward the motel. As we approached an intersection in the left hand lane, a car in the right hand lane turned left in front of us. The move startled me and I braked a little to avoid a collision though the car was several yards in front of us and the braking might not have been necessary. But then a second car started to turn. Maybe he was being led somewhere by the first and they had found themselves accidently in the wrong lane. Maybe this was some sort of Streets of San Francisco pursuit. Maybe the two cars were not associated in any way. This car was just barely ahead of us and a collision seemed eminent but the panic assisted brakes came through. There could not have been much more than the thickness of a sheet of paper between my front fender and the side of the other car when it pulled back into its lane and sped away. Seems my original plan to not drive an old car in the city at night was a good one.

We reached the motel without further incident and in the morning headed to a nearby café for breakfast. As we waited for our food, a fellow approached and asked if I was Denny Gibson. The asker turned out to be a professor from Connecticut in the area investigating colleges with his son. He eventually gave me enough clues to recognize him as someone I had met at Wigwam Village #7 in Rialto, California, in 2005. He knew of the Lincoln Highway trip from my website and put it all together when he saw someone who looked familiar. Yes, I did feel like a celebrity.

It was now time to head east. Friends familiar with the area had steered me toward Yosemite Park and Tioga Pass to start my drive home and it was a wonderful start. This was my first time ever in Yosemite where jaw dropping views surprised me around every turn. Though it was not quite as good as that in the park, more great scenery awaited me on the other side of

Yosemite rocks

Yosemite as I drove south on US 395. A stop at Manzanar, where over 11,000 Japanese-Americans were incarcerated during World War II, was both enlightening and disturbing. I toyed with the idea of turning east on US 6 from its current western terminus at Bishop, California, but decided to save that for a time when I could do the whole route and continued on to I-40 at Barstow, California.

Entrance to Manzanar

Barstow is a Route 66 town. I've driven Route 66 a few times and am quite fond of it. Knowing that I would be turning sixty-six this year, friends suggested that I should driving the road that matched my age. A 100th anniversary easily trumps a 66th birthday so a full on assault was out of the question but I could pick up a bit of the historic US route on the way home. For the next several days my path would be something of a Route 66 express. Interstate 40 would be my primary road but I would exit now and then to see particular places or people or to drive a particular section. The first one of these would occur at Kingman, Arizona.

The Valiant had flirted with overheating on the climb to Tioga Pass. It was a situation that repeated itself whenever there was a slope to climb and the ambient temperature was high. The temperature was high almost constantly and there were slopes aplenty. Staying under 50 MPH seemed to be the answer but had the side effect of often accumulating a line of cars behind me on two lane sections. Whenever that happened, I pulled over as soon as practical to let the speedier traffic pass. The flirting continued between Barstow and Kingman but, on the four-lane I-40 there was never a need to pull over to let others by. Though anti-intuitive, it seemed to be easier to drive slow on expressways than on the narrower roads.

A long stretch of old Route 66 runs between Kingman and Seligman. Leaving I-40 at Kingman to drive the old road meant that Seligman would make a good place to end the day. I called ahead to reserve a room for the night. As I approached Kingman, I used the GPS unit to search for somewhere to get my oil changed. I located a place that would not take me too far off my route and headed there.

The very young fellows who greeted me were a little unsure of what to say when they saw the old Valiant but the not quite as young manager smiled and immediately identified the car and engine. He smiled even more when he learned that I was carrying the proper oil filter with me.

The oil change went smoothly but a gas leak at the fuel pump was discovered in the process. The manager tried tightening the fittings with no effect. He called a friend who recommended a man up the road to dig deeper. I drove directly to the place recommended but the garage was closed with no one there.

I now had a decision to make. I could remain in Kingman until I found a suitable mechanic or at least a reasonable place to work on the car myself or I could drive on to Seligman. The prudent thing, of course, would have been to stay in Kingman and from my living room in Cincinnati, it is hard to understand why I didn't do just that but the fact is I drove on. I first stopped at a parts store and picked up a length of brake line since I thought that the most likely problem. Almost as an afterthought, I asked if the had a fuel pump for a 1963 Valiant. Much to my surprise and as testament to just how popular those slant sixes were, they did. I took the $19.95 pump along just in case. When a friend heard this he informed me that a clue you might be an old car nut is when you find yourself buying parts you don't need -- just in case.

The first thing I did when I arrived at the motel in Seligman was arrange for a second night. Later, when the engine had cooled down, I verified that something more than a simple tightening of fittings was required. In the morning, I got serious about finding a mechanic. When the hunt foundered, I resigned myself to another parking lot repair. As I loosened the fitting at the pump, I was struck by how poorly aligned the tubing

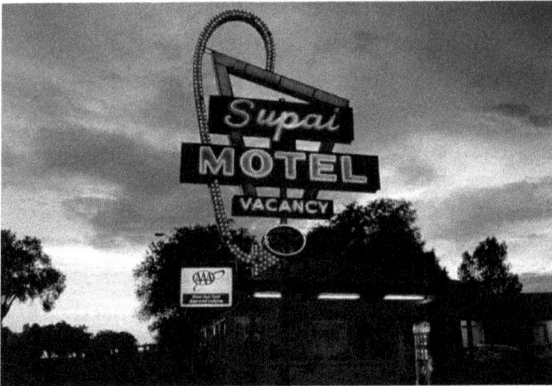

Supai Motel, Seligman, AZ

was with the fitting. I had bent the tubing so that it reached the proper points and I could tighten the fittings but it was not a very comfortable arrangement. In fact, it seemed to me that the sideways pressure of the tubing might have prevented the fitting from seating properly. I carefully bent the tubing so its tip was better aligned with the connection at the fuel pump and tightened everything down. Golly! No leaks.

I made a little test run around town and took a few top down pictures of the car in front of local businesses then buttoned it up and waited for the rain. The heavy rain that had been predicted for the afternoon appeared only a little behind schedule and made me happy to not be driving in it. It also made me happy to have a car whose fuel pump did not leak even though its window seals did.

Valiant in front of the Snow Cap, Seligman, AZ

Photographing the Valiant in front of assorted Route 66 icons would be the theme for the next few days. I doubt that I will ever again have the Valiant on the historic highway so taking all the standard tourist shots seemed just the thing to do. I posed the car at the Wigwam Village in Holbrook, Arizona, and El Rancho in Gallup, New Mexico, before stopping for the night in Albuquerque.

Wigwam Village #6
Holbrook, AZ

El Rancho
Gallup, NM

I started off the next day by heading a little north of Albuquerque to visit Tinkertown Museum. This is the motion filled folk art museum that Ross Ward built, as he liked to say, "…while you were watching TV."

Tinkertown Museum, Albuquerque, NM

I then returned to the expressway but exited to shoot the car at the Blue Swallow in Tucumcari and by what remains of the old motel sign in Glen Rio. I spent the night in Vega, Texas.

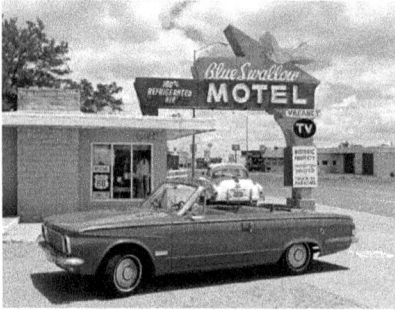

Blue Swallow Motel
Tucumcari, NM

Glen Rio, TX
A ghost town

The next day's photo ops included the U-Drop-Inn in Shamrock, Texas, the old Lucille's gas station near Hydro, Oklahoma, and Robert's Grill in El Reno. Besides snapping a few pictures at Robert's, I downed a trademark onion burger and sampled the chili.

U-Drop-Inn
Shamrock, TX

Lucille's
Hydro, OK

Robert's Grill
El Reno, OK

After a night in Stroud, Oklahoma, I got pictures of the Valiant in front of the Rock Café then went inside for breakfast and a visit with owner Dawn Welsh. Although I had eaten at "The Rock" on five previous occasions, this was my first time meeting Dawn. I don't expect it to be my last. Next up was a photo of the car at Afton Station and a visit with owner and long time friend, Laurel Kane.

Rock Café
Stroud, OK

Afton Station
Afton, OK

That was almost, but not quite, my last contact with Route 66 on the trip. Between Seligman and Oklahoma City, I had primarily

Rail Haven Motel, Springfield, MO

driven I-40 and exited to the old road for photos. At Oklahoma City, I moved onto the old two-lane and followed it through Afton. Then, a little north of Afton, I left Sixty-Six to head almost directly east on US 60. US 60 passes Springfield, Missouri, at its southern edge which was close enough to let me slip into town for a night at the Rail Haven, an historic Route 66 motel where I've long wanted to stay.

Mississippi River Bridge
Cairo, IL

Ohio River Bridge
Cairo, IL

Near Cairo, Illinois, I crossed the Mississippi and Ohio Rivers in quick succession on bridges significantly older than either car or driver. The bridge over the Mississippi was built in 1929 and the one over the Ohio in 1937. Rain hit hard near Paducah, Kentucky, which prompted me to end the day early at a nondescript motel. I spent part of the next morning getting a guided tour of Apple Valley Hillbilly Garden and Toyland Museum then crossed the Tennessee River on a 1931 bridge with a three ton limit that was closed less than a month later. Just made it.

I fueled up for the next to last time in Salem, Kentucky. Smells from a hot food counter inside the station helped me realize that I had not yet eaten anything that day so I grabbed a catfish sandwich and a bunch of fried okra. Down the road, I pulled into the empty parking lot of a pretty little white church and ate my lunch while watching some corn grow and a little traffic roll by. That "journey's end" mood, where you are ready to get home but not ready for the trip to be

Apple Valley Hillbilly Garden and Toyland Museum

Lunch break in Kentucky

over, was coming on strong. I ate slowly and took one last picture of the Valiant. I spent the last night of the trip in a Motel 6 in Owensboro.

I stayed with US 60 to Louisville then jumped onto I-71 for the run to Cincinnati. Even though the sky was cloudy, everything was dry and the drive was pleasant right up to the minute I entered my home state. As if it were triggered by me crossing the state line, the skies opened and the deluge commenced as I made my way over the bridge into Ohio. The top was up but the windows down as I and a fleet of semis navigated the multilane spaghetti through downtown Cincinnati. I heard the sound of

Cincinnati straight ahead

something hitting the car and got visual verification a short time later. Near the bottom of the windshield almost directly in front of me was a star shaped chip from what I assume was a pebble thrown by a tire on one of those semis. Less than twenty miles from home and my windshield cracks.

And that was it. That crack in the windshield was the only damage to the car during the entire trip. The failed fuel pump and the early brake light trouble were the only mechanical problems. No tires went flat, no belts broke, and no hoses leaked. There was plenty of time, 35 days, for more to go wrong. The car could have left me stranded anywhere along 7341 miles of roadway including a few that were unpaved. It could have broken down in any of 19 states. But it didn't.

The trip was everything I wanted it to be and more. Not only did the old Valiant cooperate, so did the weather. I count only six days with rain although there was some overnight precipitation a time or two. Six out of thirty-five is not at all bad especially considering that the rain usually did not last long and five of those six days occurred east of the Mississippi.

Emily Post ended *By Motor to the Golden Gate* with a detailing of expenses and a series of hand drawn maps showing each day's travel. Regarding expenses, I suppose I could produce such details but, as someone in New York said about Emily's plan to take an automobile across the country, "Why do anything so dreary?" I can however, in addition to the already mentioned states, days, and miles (19, 35, and 7341), give an accounting of gasoline and hotels. I used about 330 gallons of the former and slept in 29 of the latter with five nights in one and two nights in another. The total cost was much more than I'd have liked and much less than it was worth.

As for maps, the Lincoln Highway Association website (lincolnhighwayassoc.org) contains a complete interactive map of all known Lincoln Highway alignments. Similar maps were produced for the Centennial Tours so the route I followed along the Lincoln Highway is available. My rather haphazard routes between the Lincoln and my home seem of little value. Even if I were to "do anything so dreary" as to make them, I doubt many would "do anything so dreary" as to look at them. Emily's daily maps were preceded by a map of the United States giving an overview of her entire trip and that is something I have included at the book's beginning. It is not hand drawn, however, and for that you should be thankful. Once the trip begins, a map of the US starts each chapter with a line showing the drive covered by the chapter.

Between the expenses and the maps, Emily Post answered the question her editors sent her off with: "How far can you go in comfort?" To Emily and to those who asked the question, "comfort" meant a Pullman train car or an ocean liner cabin. The speed of passenger jets has made that sort of comfort less needed (Which is a good thing because it has also become unobtainable.) but maybe it is fair to ask, "How far can you go in comfort in an unairconditioned squeaky old car?" I don't know what the answer to that question is for the general population but I did learn that, for me, the answer is all the way to the Golden Gate -- and back.

ABOUT THE AUTHOR

Denny Gibson is a retired software engineer living on the outskirts of Cincinnati, Ohio. He is addicted to driving two-lane highways and, since 1999, has documented his travels on them at DennyGibson.com. His photographs have appeared in other travel books and the Lincoln Highway Association Forum and American Road Magazine have published his words as well as photographs. This is his first book.

www.ingramcontent.com/pod-product-compliance
Lightning Source LLC
Chambersburg PA
CBHW060209070426
42447CB00035B/2872